# RE-READING
# JAYANTA MAHAPATRA

(Selected Poems)

Edited, Compiled and a Critical Introduction
by
## Nandini Sahu

BLACK EAGLE BOOKS
2022

 BLACK EAGLE BOOKS

USA address:
7464 Wisdom Lane
Dublin, OH 43016

India address:
E/312, Trident Galaxy, Kalinga Nagar,
Bhubaneswar-751003, Odisha, India

E-mail: info@blackeaglebooks.org
Website: www.blackeaglebooks.org

First International Edition Published by
BLACK EAGLE BOOKS, 2022

**RE-READING JAYANTA MAHAPATRA**
*(SELECTED POEMS)*

Edited, Compiled and a Critical Introduction by **Nandini Sahu**

Copyright © **Jayanta Mahapatra**
Copyright of the Introduction @ **Nandini Sahu**

Cover & Interior Design: Ezy's Publication

ISBN- 978-1-64560-200-2 (Paperback)
Library of Congress Control Number: 2021943274

Printed in the United States of America

## Dedication

*To*
*Sir*
*with*
*Love*

# ACKNOWLEDGEMENTS

In my journey as a Jayanta Mahapatra researcher, there are some special persons to whom I would like to express my profound gratitude.

Late Professor Niranjan Mohanty, my guide, who introduced me to the bard.

My teacher, Professor Gopa Ranjan Mishra, who has been my co-voyager in this journey of reading Mahapatra.

My teachers and mentors—Dr. Gourishankar Hota, Prof. Himanshu Shekhar Mohapatra, Prof. E Raja Rao, Prof. Dharanidhar Sahu, Prof. Ram Narayan Panda, Dr. Chittaranjan Mishra, Prof. Sailendra Narayan Tripathy, Prof. Soubhagya Kumar Mishra, Prof. Anusuya Kumari, Dr. Bibhu Padhy, Prof. Amulya Purohit and Prof. Dilip Das.

My son, Parthasarathi Sahu, for being a patient teen-ager, who bore with all that 'obscure' poetry that I recited! And of course, for asking me tough questions. And to Sagar, Sneha, Pushpa and Devendar, for being there, like Oxygen in water.

Mr. Satya Pattanaik from Black Eagle Books, for his faith in me.

Am grateful to my dear friends Dr.Vibhuti and Dr.Prashant for reading my books with keen interest and for their honest appreciation and sensitive criticism. Many thanks to Dr. Anamika for her camaraderie.

And of course, to the poet himself--to the incredible, unparalleled Jayanta Mahapatra, who told me last week, "I know you will do my book with love, Nandini! You are too good to me!"

To which I replied, "Yes, I am."

**- Nandini Sahu**

# CONTENTS

# A Critical Introduction

## Nandini Sahu

### I

I have to, I certainly have to, share specifics of a few emotional moments I spent with poet Padma Shri Jayanta Mahapatra (b.1928) before I get into my serious academic discourse and engagement as a Jayanta Mahapatra scholar. I met 'the' Jayanta Mahapatra in 1995 for the first time in the PG Department of English, BU, Odisha, when he had come to our department to award the Gold Medal to the student with highest percentage, the Dorothy Deerings Award, and that year I, fortunately, was the awardee. I looked mesmerized at his calm, composed face without a blink, touched his feet on the dais, he blessed me graciously. The same year I stood first in the All India Poetry Contest, which he had noticed in the newspapers; and he didn't forget to congratulate me, saying, *you are small-town-simple-girl, a serious academic, and you'll see the world!* My happiness knew no bounds! Then and there I decided that I would do my PhD on his poetry, and the next day I requested my Supervisor, Late Prof. Niranjan Mohanty, to allow me to submit a synopsis on Mahapatra's poetry, which he very kindly facilitated. Rest is history. Today I can proudly say that I am a Jayanta Mahapatra scholar!

During my PhD courses, I could never meet Jayanta Sir, I only took a couple of telephonic interviews with him. After PhD I joined IACR, and then IGNOU as a professor. I guided many research scholars to write their PhD theses on Mahapatra, I introduced his poetry in many a syllabus of universities. I never forgot to mention him in my classes, as if it were my moral responsibility! Over the years, my personal relationship with Sir has evolved from a student/ researcher to daughter (even he says that I am his granddaughter!) to now almost his mother! Since last few years I treat him like my child; I pamper him, reproach him if he is careless with health or eating on time, I protect and love him. Sir gets teary eyed every time I call him to ask after his health and wellbeing. Three years ago I visited him at Tinikonia Bagicha with Gopa Sir (Prof. Gopa Ranjan Mishra); he was overwhelmed to see me. I had taken a bunch of silver lemon-chilies (*Nimbu-Mirchi)* for him. He asked, "why did you bring this Nandini? Though they are so beautiful and artistic." I said, "See, you are so handsome, no one should cast an evil eye on you. This will protect you." His was beaming with happiness and asked Sarojini Didi (his help) to hang the *Nimbu-Mirchi* at the front door immediately. He is such. A simple man, a molten man, a pure soul, a jubilant persona with childlike virtues. He simply trusts. I remember, before Covid days, I was supposed to share the dais with him in a Lit Fest. Sir was hungry, but most of his fans were busy clicking selfies with him to post on social media. I asked him to eat before the session, but the Chinese food elaborately served on the menu, wasn't fit for a person of his age. I requested the organizers to arrange fruit salads or some simple dal-rice. But as expected, people were too busy. I left my session, went to one of my teacher's place and got a piece of *Podapitha* (fermented rice-black gram-cake with grated coconut). By the time I came, the session was over and he was still sitting hungry. Seeing the *Podapitha*, he was teary-eyed. While eating the cake, he told me that this is his favorite dish. I can just go on talking about how much he loves me and my son Parthasarathi. This year when he got Covid, I was shattered, I myself was on the covid bed in Delhi. I called up every possible source in Odisha to arrange support for Sir; a couple of my poet friends coordinated and Sir was in safe hands. He recovered, bounced back with his energy and good health. I apprehend, no, I am convinced, a Jayanta Mahapatra is born only once in millenniums, to enrich the civilization with poetry and limpidness.

This book has always been at the back of my mind for last two decades, and I unsuccessfully attempted a couple of times to make a complete Jayanta Mahapatra Reader. But everything happens when time is ripe for it, and everything happens for good. That is why Mr. Satya Pattanaik, the erudite publisher of Black Eagle Publications, facilitated me to do this book at this point of my life when there is an emotive helix and a mellifluous ringlet flowing melodiously between Jayanta Sir and me. In fact, the entire Indian English literary fraternity loves him and is indebted to him for creating the historiography of Indian English poetry where we safely, cozily, comfortably belong. This book is the tribute, highest respect, from a young poet to a senior poet, from a devotee to divinity incarnate, idol embodied. This book is my admiration, highest respect, to my rich pedigree, to the historiography of Indian English poetry I belong to, shaped by the doyen like poet Jayanta Mahapatra.

## II

Jayanta Mahapatra is a poet of remarkable power and vision and he has made his mark on the passage of Indian English poetry. His book *Relationship* brought him the honour of Sahitya Akademi Award in 1980, which was the first honour ever given to a book of poetry in Indian writing in English. Though Mahapatra is a near contemporary of established Indian English poets like Ezekiel and Ramanujan, his creative career started rather late. Although he is the first Indian English poet to have received the Sahitya Akademi Award, majority of his initial poems were published in American journals and literary magazines. His first poem was accepted in *South and West*, a literary magazine in the USA. *Close the Sky, Ten by Ten* (1971), his first collection of poems, was published by Dialogue Publications, Calcutta, but received punitive reviews from Indian reviewers. Anyway, American readers were convivial to his poetry at that point. Ronald Bayes, editor of St Andrews Review, North Carolina, gave him a promising review. To quote Mahapatra's words regarding Bayes, "There was compassion in Bayes's review, and understanding – something, once again, I found absent in my Indian reviewers."

Afterwards, Robert Buffington, the editor of the University of Georgia Press, fortified him to send him a manuscript. His poetry manuscript, titled *A Rain of Rites*, was, in the following year, selected for publication in the university's Poetry Series. And within a year, other American journals like New York Quarterly, Poetry (Chicago), The Sewanee Review and The New Republics, New Yorker, Poetry International, Tri Quarterly, The Kenyon Review, World Literature Today, Chicago Review, The Hudson Review, New Letters, International Quarterly, Poetry(Chicago), Boundary and other international platforms accommodated his poems.

Mahapatra was awarded the significant Jacob Glatstein Memorial Prize in the year 1975 for the eleven poems published in the journal *Poetry*. He was then invited to Iowa as a Visiting Writer from India in the International Writing Program for the year 1976-77. The trip Mahapatra took to the U.S.A, changed the sequence of his poetic career. The experience he attained after his conference with some notable writers helped him build a niche for himself. He read poetry at the University of the South at Sewanee and also at St Andrew's College in Laurinburg, and Montgomery College in Washington D.C. In his later visits to the USA, he had readings at Hunter College, New York, Narope Institute in Boulder, Colorado, and at the International Museum of World Folk Art, La Jolla. After the publication of the long poem "Relationship" by Greenfield Review Press, US, in 1980, Vernon Young appreciated Mahapatra in a review published in The Hudson Review. He finally received the National Academy of Letters Award, New Delhi, in 1981.

The Indian English poetry situation was riddled with unsolved contradictions and uncertainties when Mahapatra started writing. Even today, the Indian English poet has to express in a tongue that is not his/her own, an experience that is personal and an ethos that is alien to the language.

Mahapatra is aware of the uncertainties, and he said in an interview, "I have to pull the words out of my veins with my sweat and my tears. It is not an easy thing for me to do."[1] Anyway, the despair of the creative activity does not get reflected in his poetry. He is not at all self-conscious in his use of foreign tongue which becomes malleable in his hands. The creative activity evolves for Mahapatra reaching out to the silence in the mind where the poet and the expression meet, merge and dissolve and also reach out from the silence in all world orders. He says:

> What appears to disturb me is the triumph of silence in the mind, and if these poems are inventions, they are also longings amid the flow of voices towards a need that I feel is defensive. A poem makes me see out of it in all directions, like a sieve, and I am almost relieved at that all important thought.[2]

This explains the quality of tranquility and quietude about his poetry. It is true that Mahapatra's poetry celebrates past and the nostalgic elements are strewn over his poetry. Yet it would not be possible to accept him as a Romantic, as he is not prepared to accept the expertise of imagination— the central instrument of the poetics of the Romantics. His poetry reveals a self that is secluded and withdrawn. Apart from the poet's personal loss or pain, there are three reasons for his isolation. Firstly, because the poet is more sensitive than any other man, is patently aware of the contemporary milieu or situation; secondly, he himself as well as others feel that he moves ahead of time; and thirdly, rather more emotionally, he is not happy in the present, and the present is not promising for him. His mind lurks in the past in quest of something that he himself is not aware of. He lags behind time and is thus remote. But there are exceptions too, like Wallace Stevens, whose refusal to idolize the stale past introduces to his note of affirmation. He believes, like Eliot, the past that hangs over us like the king's familiar sword is far more meticulous and demanding, and hence it is nauseating and fabricating. Stevens attacked our romantic favor of the past. One must detach oneself even from the minds of the contemporaries so far as they carry the past to the vanguard. Stevens argues further for the newness of forms since the present can be relied upon and thus the past loses all its energy for him. But most unlikely, Jayanta Mahapatra's recollective mode has a great implication in his poetry. Past, both familial / personal and cultural / historical, silhouette his thoughts. The object of this book is to analyze how familial as well as racial past serve as a mode to redemption in the poet's heart, while re-reading some of the famous poems of Mahapatra. His family, father, mother, grandfather, son and at the same time Odishan culture, the Konark temple, Emperor Asoka, Kalinga War, Cuttack, Bhubaneswar, and India at large, are the topics of his poetry. Again, the reason behind his desperate inclination towards the past is something about rereading the poet. The poet has always been a lover of memory, recollection, past, may be because he is afraid of the fleeting nature of time, afraid of death, unhappy with the contemporary society, with his own self because of the personal losses, or may be because he has a quest to know his roots. The choice of the creative medium (English) also coerces him to register and affirm his identity, as an Odia, and an Indian. He celebrates the stories associated with the place he is born into with a view to authenticating his identity. His grandfather's acceptance of Christianity years ago and the poet's love of Hindu culture, tradition at present may be cited as another reason of his quest for roots, hence a temptation towards the past. Reading his past is re-reading him per se!

Mahapatra began his poetic career as a poet of love. His earlier poetry tried to capture the multiple facets of love, so as to relate it to the evocative conformation of life. Moments of richer antagonism, separation, meeting and temporary misunderstandings which contribute to the fruition of love make him aware of the seminal needs of the mortals. As a poet of love in his early poetry Mahapatra tried to capture the multiple facets of love, so as to relate it to the meaningful conformation of life. It is only in his early poetry that one discovers an increasing awareness of the fleeting nature of time and of the gift of the past as a priceless possession. In a candid confession he writes: "Yes, I ruefully admit, my first poems were born of love, of love's selfishness, and of a huge self-pity, like the poems of many I admire."[3]

Even if Mahapatra is 'rueful' about his beginning as a love poet, yet it is through his love poetry that he could learn how to establish a rapport with the past or tradition or culture in his later poetry. His poetry has been gradually the poetry of withdrawal into the self where it is almost itself, unadorned, moving and still, sans pretense and insincere masks. This willingness to delve deep into the archetypal fabric of the living becomes a connection between Mahapatra's early poetry and later. The pursuit for the self has given an emblem of continuity to his poetry. Refinement sophistication in terms of articulation and organization of world and experiences, of feeling and sensations have added a startling sense of newness to his poetry. As one moves from his early to later poetry one observes a change in the treatment of themes, a shift in the style quite unassuming and devoid of any auras of experimentation. But even if he has matured, what remains striking and evident is the nature of his self. A note of pessimism is available from his early to later poetry.

The forlorn memorandum in Mahapatra's poetry is an outcome of several motives. In a good number of poems, he celebrates his family and at places tries to relate himself to the discernable and indiscernible dimensions of the home or family or its members living or dead with a view to the crucial  pursuit for that root and his own identity. Home, therefore, assumes a staggering amount of space in his poetry. It has both positive and adverse sides. As long as it reinforces the poet's identity and saves him from the loss of an aspect, and as long as it becomes an absolute link between past, present and future, and he does not shrink back from rejoicing home as a gifted metaphor. But at the same time, he is cognizant of the changes, the losses which sneak into the family slowly in order to cause or create deep lesions of loneliness in him. In a poem "Silence in the Village", the poet attempts to know the reasons of this melancholy:

> Do I detect a note of melancholy in my voice?
> No use explaining that my life
> has involved me in delicate situations
> for which solutions could not be found.
>
> (*A Whiteness of Bone*, 1)

The nefariousness of loss which Mahapatra experiences and elucidates in his poetry branches partly from the past and partly from the present. It stems from the past because it materialized or occurred once and it cannot be accomplished again, except for in memory. It stems from the present because of the realization that the present is barren of any functioning systems or ethics.

Besides, he comes across loneliness, betrayal, hunger, poverty, violence, disease and death ubiquitously. In trying to seek redemption from the disease-ridden present, he falls back on the history. His acute pangs of loneliness originate from the loss of childhood, of father, mother, grandfather and above all, of his innocence. In "Grand Father" Mahapatra holds his grandfather accountable for the pessimism in the family because of his absence. His grandfather embraces Christianity during the terrible famine that struck Odisha in 1866. The reawakening of the memories of his grandfather through the yellow diary becomes both a mien of joy and sorrow, joy because the poet could hold it sincerely, sadness because the grandfather is absent forever:

> The yellowed diary's notes whisper in vernacular.
> The sound the forgotten posture,
> the cramped cry that forces me
> to hear that voice.
> Now I stumble in your block-paged wake.
>
> (*Life Signs*, 20)

The poet, in the absence of his grandfather, regrets that he should have known him more intimately and closely even in his absence. The grandfather blesses the poet and his family, and the poet himself is lucky enough to recognise the glories of heritage:

> A conscience of years is between us.
> He is young.
> The whirls of glory are breaking down
> for him before me.
> Does he think of the past, as a loss
> we have lived, out own ?
> Out of silence we look back now at what
> we do not know.

There is a dawn waiting beside us, whose signs
are a hundred odd years away from you,
Grandfather.

(*Life Signs*, 20)

In 'The Way of the River' the poet tries to collect the pebbles of his identity following the slow flow of the river across the sal and deodar jungle of the ancestral past. While moving across the banks he realised that his existence would have gathered no meaning without the blessings of his father and forefathers:

Tonight I know that the life I have lived
is my life softened in my father's life ...
I am the water in any father's eyes
I am the slow flow that takes me
gently down.

(*Life Signs*, 21)

A sense of loss and isolation become touching in the absence of his father. He recollects richly the changes between his time and his father's, between himself and his father:

My old father believes, even in his last days,
that's why he isn't a lover or a poet.
He cannot drown himself in water
or in awe.

(*A Whiteness of Bone*, 2)

In "Consolations" the poet falls back on the memories of his dying father. He is certain that there is no escape either from past, agony or from death:

I remember my father, dying
under the slackening kindness of librium,
making pained noises, reaching out
his life to fill my tongue and mouth
with the bitter taste of despair.

The other dead are so quiet.
And one feels no more than
a passing shadow of shame
When one remembers them.

(A Whiteness of Bone, 4)

Like us, did you feel you were going into death
through fear of death?
Thinking to escape it as we go to meet it?

In fear of suffering, I come to you,
because here is death, and nothing to see.
You've moved away from your past,
lonely in your death, to show us
how necessary it is for us too, to die alone,
Each one, everything, every being,
all alone before nothingness, today, tomorrow.

(Sky without Sky, VI)

The poet recollects that his old father was unable to break the bondage with home that was established once. Even in death his father shares the son's suffering and sympathizes:

And through the dull suburbs
of his death, my old father
gropes his way back;
Yes, he seems to whisper
overwhelmed by the defeat
in my eyes, hunger and earth
made the bones of one's breath.

(A Whiteness of Bone, 4)

And he remembers every detail of his father:

My father, teetotaler, vegetarian,
took two baths a day,
one at dawn the other

before his evening obeisance
to Lord Shiva at the temple.

(*A Whiteness of Bone*, 5)

It is relevant in this context to evoke what Mahapatra wrote about his father in an autobiographical and reflective essay:

My father worked as a sub-inspector of primary schools and his earnings were comparatively meagre. Father's work kept him away from home. It would be right to say, however, that there was a strong and warm bond between us, and that this lasted right until his death. That was a little more than two years ago. Perhaps as emotional involvements usually are, something in the way a father reaches for his son's hand, with a vague longing that life should last forever, I remember the web of force, the silence of which we are a recognizable part. These times protected me with courage."[4]

In "Orissa Landscape", the poet fondly recollects a moment when he cut his chin his mother came worried and pressed sugar against the wound to check the bleeding. For the poet, blood is not blood, it is the ooze of love:

A long time ago
I cut my chin and bled.
My mother clumsily held a lump of sugar
against the wound
to stop the ooze of love.

Mahapatra's commitment for the past, his fidelity to the heritage and flow of legacy are so deep delved that even in misery and helplessness, he sheds warm tears like his 'father's child'. In the galaxy of his familial past, not only father, but also grandfather, mother, younger brother, and culture, tradition at large, shine like stars to ease him in the darkness of the present. Amorak Huey views in an article titled "Claiming a Language : Writing India into English : A Review" that "With such large, overwhelming themes, Mahapatra runs the risk of allowing his poetry to become overlay, abstract and sentimental, but his photographic eye for detail prevents this. His poetry is a graceful blend of minute and abstraction, detail and speculation."[6] The poet recapitulates the memories of his younger brother and mother:

> Tonight
> the shadow of my brother follows me,
> becoming blood in its hooves.
> My loving brother turns pale and cross.
>
> (*A Whiteness of Bone*, 3)

He recollects the pain his mother had to consume. His sympathies with the aged mother make him a silent part of the life lost beyond reminiscence:

> In this room of mine
> last year's calendar hangs uselessly on the wall.
> In my mother's eyes pain begins to stir again
> like a venerable old gentleman
> who has returned from afar.
>
> (*A Whiteness of Bone*, 15)

Setting alone in a gelid December dawn, the poet recollects his mother and compares his own sadness with his mother's:

> The old woman
> with gray hair and coarse wrinkled hands
> Whom I call mother looks vacantly into her
> tea cup, things she has been betrayed.
>
> (*A Whiteness of Bone*, 24)

Remembering the flash of whiteness of emotions and

whispers of loneliness that surrounded his house and the changed mother, the poet's heart becomes heavy:

> But what I realize is that
> before I reach the door
> it would have all turned white
> Mother stands by the door
> still wearing her clothes of mourning
> I don't remember what father's
> death was like.
>
> (*A Whiteness of Bone,* 29)

The poet couriers an unsuccessful attempt to do away with the past. It may be because of the fact that the past is the obligation of infinite pains and anguishes. He falls back on the house that sheltered him once:

> There is a photograph still hanging
> on the wall in my father's house. It is quite old,
> and against an elaborate
> backdrop the photographer used
> are my parents, my younger brother and I.
> I want to shut it from my mind
> because it reminds one of a useless monument.
>
> (*A Whiteness of Bone,* 29)

Perhaps with a deep sense of sullenness the poet intends to disinherit the past. If it were his real intentions, he wouldn't have expressed his willingness to protect and presume the past in the closet of his heart:

> Now with what longings
> shall I protect my memory ?
>
> (*A Whiteness of Bone,* 43)

But had the poet sincerely wished to dismiss his past, he would not have maintained a reverential stance. He is painfully aware of the changes which have crept into his life. In this changed world, he realizes that his mother would have proved herself a nonconformist. The poet's sympathies with the mother are innate:

> Dear mother, your time is not come
> and the sun is swarming all over the day.
> We shall watch you run, mother,
> Until you realize you fit in nowhere,
> through little bits of your life,
> Your weakness
> as you startle at every step
> by the daughters of children
> in the rustle of your petticoats.
>
> (*A Whiteness of Bone*, 48)

The July rains, the heavy clouds in the expansive blue make the poet lonelier than isolation. He recollects the old house where he spent his childhood:

> The old brick walls of my house
> go down into shadow.
> I remember tales prattled,
> My grandfather's ghost standing in the rain
> watching the secrets between us burn away
> And smoke past his grey eyes;
> Mother's voice a cricket's scream
> and my remorse, like the brief red glow
> of fireflies, gashing the air of the trees.
>
> (*A Whiteness of Bone*, 39)

In 'The Naked Light', the poet fondly recollects his mother:

> My mother's voice trembles quietly
> in the backyard among uneven grasses.
> And when all reason for trusting the stars
> has gone, I find my own place here,
> the naked light unable to draw me into it.
>
> (*A Whiteness of Bone*, 48)

But unexpectedly, one can discern a changed attitude in the poet's writings by comparing these mother poems with his autobiographical notes. He admits that the relationship with his mother was a strained one:

I have never been able to feel that affinity with mother as I had with mother. She was erotic in her ways and as I grew up, my conflicts with her increased. She was shrewd, ingenious, believing in anything she heard, even total strangers. So often I longed for someone in whom I could confide, like a sister or cousin of my age but this did not come about. Mother's rantings went on, if according to her, something had not gone on her way. I too never put in an attempt to explain my behaviour if I believed there had been no slips on my side. Right and wrong, good and evil—she filed these thoughts, all acts, into closed drawers of her life. I was flushed with a constant tension. I didn't know what was important to me anymore. It made me veer away from the flow of blame and liability that life must want us to have at times. I slipped into dreams.[7]

But the possible reason behind this changed attitude may be that Mahapatra had started using a persona in order to sustain a distance from his own subjective self. This appears more germane because Mahapatra who lives in three layers of time—the mythical, the historical and the contemporary—bears a propensity to mythicize his own past in order that it might allocate universality and impartiality to his erudite art. It remains crystal clear and reliable from his poetry that his veneration for and faith in the past is deep rooted and redeeming. This is exactly why recollection serves as a mode of redemption for him.

As a complement to and proof of fitting into the past that lies in his poetry, the complex poet remembers his old house that had given him a relaxed solitude once. With the passing of time, the willingness to whirl back to infancy becomes stronger:

> This house, my room, yesterday's flowers,
> there are corners my hands never touched.
> Once I touched a woman here,
> her breath warm as loo that blows in Summer
> who could think them
> that the lonely body held so much of blood ?
> on room's west wall
> the white of a photograph's flight
> has dulled slowly into grimy brown.
> A breath that trembles in a spider wed there
> could bear witness to my faith in love as memory,
> held as I am here by a fear creeping
> along the skin.
> Light tricks, revealing
> unknown bones of the air.
> In the house I figure the possibilities of life.
> Could I hide again as a child, some place here ?
> The woman in the silent frame before me
> does not stir. Old murmurs
> wear me out again.
> And I suppose I must have loved.
> As I look out, I realize sadly,
> our sons are with us too.
>
> (*A Whiteness of Bone*, 22)

Reading these lines one may say here Mahapatra epitomizes a precise family album, injured by the fierce talons of time with its subdued passing. The desolation of the poet stems from the recollection of the lost youth rather than from the existence of two sons who remind of the poet the changing designs of time. His account of the house in his autobiographical essay makes clear our consideration of the poet's deep sense of allegiance to it:

> The house where I grew up in Cuttack was located at one end of a cluster of houses ... The house of my childhood turned into a strange intense memory in later years. This was the one father built into which we moved when I was nearly six. Father had left for the interior province, and we lived by ourselves alone. The nights were uncertain, and I recollect barring the front and back doors without fail before the onset of darkness every evening. A dismal setting indeed, and one which haunted me with a certain persistence—until years later a day came when I decided to put the whole thing on a paper in an exercise of exorcism ... So this house of mind became substance as did my mother, physically ill with the passage of time, moving back and forth in the restless darkness, my younger brother at his heals. We had no electricity in the house (it was luxury for us), and the long veranda with its adjoining courtyard seemed to float about in a ghostly light, filling me with a sense of necessity— I could not overcome.[8]

Recollection helps as a mode of redemption to Mahapatra in the logic that whirling back to the place of his birth and childhood has become a passion that keeps him away from the fear of being anonymous in this swarming cosmos. In 'December' he makes this passion explicit:

To live one must do these things one loves,
but always in secret. So to keep going
back to the place one has come from.

(A Whiteness of Bone, 24)

In trying to disown his house, the poet clings to it intimately:

Once there was more to this than meets my eye;
the beamed roof of the house,
the veranda
the pitchers of waters for us to drink
a lantern's light and rest in someone's eyes
leaving over the night.

(A Whiteness of Bone, 29)

The poet's untarnished love for and admiration to his ancestral familial past constitute for him a cocoon to which often he retires in order to dismiss the burdens of isolation, fears of ageing and death. The poet's desire to flow down the bank of ancestral past remainders for him a persistent motif which rejuvenates and substantiates his identity. In "Way of the River" the poet celebrates his identify, following the slow flow of the river across *sal* and *deodar*. While concentrating over the private past, the poet often is swayed towards the cultural past. He transports himself from the macrocosm of the private self to the macrocosm of the home, and through such transference and transcendence the poet tries to categorize himself with his roots, evidencing that he 'contains multitudes'.

The poems of Jayanta Mahapatra are haunted by a love of India. Mahapatra is very much aware of his country's history, and in the poems, he explores this history, rewrites, enriches it. It is a colossal task he has set himself, and it often leaves the poet dismayed, troubled. In the first lines of "Silent in the Valleys", he writes:

The world is full of toys, many of them unused.
Do I detect a note of melancholy in my voice ?
No use explaining that my life
has involved me in delicate situations
for which solutions could not be found.

(A Whiteness of Bone, 1)

A note of melancholy remains in Mahapatra's voice throughout, but it never gets in his way, never drags his poems down into the sentimental world of oblivion:

... We have hung out
the carcass of the past in cross roads
our children keep seeing
our fingers pulling shreds of meat from it.

(A Whiteness of Bone, p.45)

Most of the poems are not exercises in exorcism of the poet's own culpability; like Greek tragedies their bearings are cathartic, generating a sense of empathy in the readers. In "Unreal Country", where memory is the theme, the poetic persona becomes the meeting ground of time past represented by the dead father and the future represented by the son, 'searching for stars still'. The present is caught between the past disillusionments and future longings—a present which is 'overwhelmed by the defeat' that he comes across time and again. About the presence of the cultural past in *A Whiteness of the Bone*, D.B. Pattnaik writes in an article "Presence of the Past":

The poems in the collection will endure for the challenge they pose to out-cultural moorings and the alternative they offer for a way of living. The challenge is for us to shed our apathy and broaden our consciousness. The time tested

Indian stoic and contemplative virtue of pity, compassion and endurance is offered as a heroic alternative to the current western action ethic. The poems are a true reflection of the synthesis Mahapatra's own society is seeking through the contradictions which the forces of history have presented it with.[9]

"The past / lies everywhere, like water,", says Mahapatra in his poem "Afternoon" (AWOB,10). The present which seldom comforts him, seems to be a sheer support system to reach back to the past. "How the earth keeps turning to my empty years," he says, "Let not my memory be like a tiger in ambush" (*A Whiteness of Bone*, 31). On some extraordinary instances he shifts from the normal melancholic brooding to the verge of wistfulness. In "Landscape" he says:

> I remember now it was an evening, in
> some past childhood,
> when we came close to each other.
> And white sails unfurled over the water,
> the scent of ceremonies
> All that one, answered with a smile.

> (*A Whiteness of Bone*, 67)

In certain poems, like "At the Summer Palace of Tipu Sultan" cultural past is the fundamental theme. The poem ends on a note with history and Seringapatam holding on to the image of Tipu and "the slack, spiritless drum holding its sounds/just as night condemned to hold on to its theme" (AWOB, 67). Thus, some of his poems stay high up on a strong outpouring of feelings, sketches from the landscape and the pain and tragedy of the people. Ultimately it is a poetry about silence and time. Keki N. Daruwalla comments:

Mahapatra is a melancholic, ruminating, modern day dervish, dancing almost in slow motion, his eye taking in every sombre tint, his mind focused on memory.[10]

The poetry of Jayanta Mahapatra is very much down-to-earth, the themes being current life conditions. He himself says, "These poems are just attempts of mine to hold a handful of earth to my face and let it speak ... Perhaps this signifies a return to my roots so that they reveal who I am."[11] In some of his poems Mahapatra sounds enormously involved with the common man, his problems, his hunger for bread and the uncaptured soul. The Odishan landscape, places in the land come out to be the periodic themes of his pen. The background of Cuttack is brought out in a poem "Again, One Day, Walking by the River"; the poet writes about the four female labourers mending a road at two o'clock in the hot summer afternoon:

A tar dim shoulders in front of the judge's house
as four women workers rub
the hot tar on to the pitted face of the road.
Soon, it will be late in the afternoon
the mangled lepers will shuffle along, going home,
their helpless looks drawing fantasies
on the town square.

(*Life Signs*, 39)

And regarding hunger, he writes:
There are two hungers, hunger for bread
And hunger for the uncouth soul
For the light's grace. I have seen both,
And chosen for an indulgent world's
Ear the story of one whose hands
Have bruised themselves on the locked

doors of life; whose heart fuller than mine
of gulped tears, is the dark well
From which to draw, drop after drop,
The terrible poetry of his kind.

(Waiting, 5)

Both the hungers—hunger for bread and hunger of the rude soul for the light's grace—can be seen and experienced in Mahapatra's poetry. The poet has perceptions of mythical, modern and cosmic worlds because his roots, his past lie in these places. The culture, rich tradition of Odisha, the devotion of the Odia people for the living Lord Jagannath have always inspired Mahapatra. The poet writes, "The sacred deity of Jagannath at Puri is fashioned from the wood of a neem tree chosen from the dance Orissa jungles every twelve years."[12] This echoes his quest for the rich cultural past of Hinduism, though the poet happens to be a Christian. Lord Jagannath is the Lord God and Protector of the world. The dense forest from which the Lord springs into life is the originator of life. The poet's consciousness, enriched by such perception, tries to touch his ultimate metaphysical conjectural roots. His Odisha has had an ancient history and culture but this history has had the knowledge of deep pain, and the pain is predominantly acute at present. In the following lines in *Relationship*, Mahapatra puts together the metamorphosis of primeval rocks into the soil of Odisha in the course of geological changes on the one hand, and, on the other, the reeking waters of the Daya river when thousands of Odias were massacred on its banks in the year 261 B.C. during King Ashoka's Kalinga campaign. He says, 'it is hard to tell'

How the age old proud stones
lost their strength and fell,

and how the waters of the Daya
stank with the bodies of my ancestors.

(*Relationship*, 14)

A preoccupation with the past and the problems of coming to terms with it seems to be the dominant motif which enlightens the poetry of Jayanta Mahapatra and controls all its varying moods. His poetry unravels a fabric of the past, woven with a few relevant historical details of the land of Odisha and its "rains everywhere/holding dim interiors of myth" (*Relationship*, 5), and the rites and rituals centered on the three temples at Bhubaneswar, Puri and Konark symbolizing an ancient tradition of which he is an inheritor. This concern with the history is the natural consequence of an awareness of the passage of time, which is revealed in his concentrated undergoing of clock time as days, nights and periods, which is very Eliotian. It is quite significant that some of his poems are titled "The Morning", "Night Fall", "Afternoons", "Dusk", "Another Evening", "The Day", "A Saturday Afternoon", "A Rain", "Summer", "Indian Summer Poem", "The Earth of July", each one of which becomes a contemplation on the routes of time. At times witnessing the channels of time suggests tender, private memories and the recognition of the pervasive loss and death of near and dear ones. Thus an October evening becomes "a time for measuring an indefatigable memory" (*The False Start*, 19) of the beloved ones whose absence fills him with agony:

Can grief let me do what I wish,
littering every corner of this dark
with awakenings of death?

(*The False Start*, 19)

Apart from such dexterous and reminiscent pictures of clock time linked with personal experience, there are poems which are exclusively deep reveries on time. On such junctures the poet adopts a voice of modesty, "The humility of the fallen trees", and tries to discover the meaning of the vast silences of the sky. He feels time drawing in:

> Time draws in timidly
> each weakness, each fear to clear focus.

(The False Start, 34)

And man's inability to contend with time is acknowledged:

> No flesh can cover the time—darkened bone
> that is there, strong enough to
> knock one's fear.

(The False Start, 36)

As is characteristic of his poetry, Mahapatra ruminates in a cluster of questions:

> How many thousand ways are there
> to take the chains of memory away.

(The False Start, 35)

and,

> What can anyone do to claim his freedom ?

(The False Start, 36)

The many false starts in life have left sad fragments at the cross-roads, and the loss of innocence, and the fall from grace have left only 'the area of shadows'… 'dripping with the blood of the perfumed voices of living'. Mahapatra's concept of time certainly resembles that of Eliot. The smaller divisions of time, days and nights, and seasons which pass by making the poet "aware of edges of our embraces", congeal into a past— personal, racial, and national—and that is what, according to him, is inherited as tradition:

> And every part of time
> will go out quietly
> into the distant hills and the stones

folding itself
in the lazy shapes of sleep.
                    (*Waiting*, 19)

The poet explores his inexhaustible theme of the past, tradition, and his relationship with it, and each poem becomes a crafty distinction on this theme. He is an Odia first, and an Indian next, and for him the past is explicit as the past of his land and his people. The past is seen in the spaces of temples and the icons, the ritual adorations and festivals, the legends and myths of the land. The Odisha landscape, the temples at Puri or Konark and their ruins convey a sense of ageing and of the passage of the inexorable time. These historic details about the land and its people are nimbly interlaced with the description of the environment, which makes one feel the weight of the past and the tradition. Mahapatra remarked in his speech made on the eve of his accepting the Sahitya Akademi award. "To Orissa, to this land in which my roots lie and lies my past, and in which lie my beginning and end ... I acknowledge my debt and relationship."[13] The main theme of his contemplation seems to be the disparity between the Orissa that was, and the Orissa that is. The grandeur of the past of Orissa has to be recreated from the ruined architecture and his legacy of the past "haunts him and puzzles him" as a reviewer of his poetry puts it.

The poet sculpts the relevant details of the land, historical and cultural, to shape an icon of the past as:

...the cruelties
of ruthless emperors who carved peaceful edicts
on blood-red rook
and the maritime glory of his people
the sailing ships of those maritime ancestors

who have vanished in the black Bay
without a trace ...

(Relationship, 10)

Again the poet comments on the past of Odisha as:
Of broken empires and of
vanquished dynasties
and of ahimsa's whimpers.

(Relationship, 34)

The past is built up of moving legends too, which becomes part of the inheritance of the poet. For instance, the legend of:

the first woman, like Topoi
on which the long heroic song
plucks the everlasting starts.

(Relationship, 12)

As much as the history of Odisha, the culture of the land haunts the poet. The ruins of the temple are the remnants of the glorious culture of the past and "Stone is the theme" as the poet puts it, in Bhubaneswar. With the red sandstone walls of Konark, Bhubaneswar and Puri, the numerous rites and rituals, the shrines and ikons, the chariot festival and Shiva worship, all described with subtle and gentle irony. He evokes the local culture of the people, with their small faiths and innumerable fetishes. The one aspect of the cultural heritage of his native land is that he is never tired of portraying the religious rituals and worship in these temples. An exceptionally beautiful picture of the ritual worship is seen in the poem 'At a Ritual Worship on a Saturday Afternoon':

Smug people about me,
drawing something out of stone
Dark quirky bodies
Crouched in the sad smears of vermillion.

(Waiting, 40)

But he is uncertain about his total engrossment in this heritage. Questions like:

What have I run out of ?
An inheritance ?
(*Waiting*, 40)

And such questions lead to irony upon the deadness of the rites and the blind faith in them:

Everywhere, an ancient rite of dead years
makes its obeisance to life.
(*Waiting*, 15)

The constant rumination over these features of the past and tradition seem to be an attempt to outline his place, milieu and his attitudes towards these. In the process of defining his relationship with this historical and cultural past, the poet begins by looking back at his personal past. Every feature of the landscape and the social life, of his land, be it "the way of the river", or "the chariot festival at Purl", reminds him of his ancestors and his deeply-felt affinity with them. He acknowledges his heritage thus:

Tonight I know that the life I have lived
is my life softened in my father's life. (*Waiting*, 10)
and
I am the water in my father's eyes.
(*Waiting*, 11)

Walking on the banks of the river, the poet remembers his ancestors:

Did a shadow
of kinship with them fall silently through
the night ?
(*Waiting*, 10)

This makes him understand the cyclic time:

Is this how a journey ends, simply to begin again ?
(*Waiting*, 10)

and strengthens his conviction regarding his roots.
This is the town where I was born ; here with others
year after year I celebrate the joyous festivals.

(*Waiting,* 27)

All these nuances and overtones of the consciousness
of time and past develop into a fine orchestration in the
poetry of Mahapatra, the final of which is struck in his
*Relationship.* About *Relationship,* C.C.L. Jayaprada views:

Relationship' is not a poem about the relationship of
a man to men in friendship, love, family or community. It
is about a relationship of man to time, man to land and
man to generations of men who have passed before him
and who will come after him. Finally, it is the relationship
of man to his self and man to his soul.[14]

In the poem, personal experience, racial consciousness
and the myth of the land intertwine with each other. In the
long poem of 12 sections the mood, with a wavelike motion,
swing between tranquility and despair, peace and defeat,
stillness and disorder. There is a constant interface between
his inner landscape and exterior landscape, between the
past and the present. The ruins of Konark and Puri, the
river Daya where king Asoka transformed to Buddhism
after the bloodbath of a dibrach victory, are persuasive and
are partakers in the racial understanding of the poet. Rock
and water, sun and rains, moonlight and darkness are
repeated images in the poem and bring the theme forward
in a web-like connotation. As he contemplates at the temple
3rd century B.C. when Asoka invaded Kalinga, and the
temple itself fuses with all the ancient temples of Odisha —
and all these fuse into one entity, the ancient culture of
Odisha. He then becomes aware that although a child of
this civilization, he is an expatriate and a pariah, with no
apparent hope of ever bridging the chasm that divides him

from his origin and ancestry. Soon from the anguished sense of alienation to which he has seemed to be permanently condemned, the narrator is able, by steady contemplation of the ruins and what they might mean, to find his way to civilization of his rootedness in, and oneness with, the civilization of his forefathers. *Relationship* is, thus, recognized by him as a major poem which deals with his relationship with the culture and tradition of India, especially of Odisha, its architectural excellence and its mythological motifs. The poem celebrates myth and history, faith and fantasy, commonplace chores and rampant charismas of the land of his birth. The poet calls it "the theme song of my life" (*Relationship*, 16).

The opening section begins by recalling the 1,200 artisans who built the temple, and the ships which made Kalinga a maritime power. The artisans are dead and separated from the narrator by an "infinite distance" and the ships "have vanished in the Black Bay without a trace" ( 1). Time cannot speak, it "has no mouth", and "the black labyrinth of casuarinas along the edges of the sea / closes the sky's eternal vault." The poet depicts the elevated culture of Odisha:

Time
and the boat
and the initiating into the mystery of peace,
the sailing ships of those maritime ancestors
who have vanished in the black Bay
without a trace
that only live in the sound of the waves
fillings themselves into the dark fringes
of this land from Chilika to Chandipur.

(*Relationship*, 10)

The second section of *Relationship* takes one to the

family through the window of the mother's grave, which evokes the memories of the white terraces of the poet's childhood. His memory awakens inside him a lost world of seclusion and hunts to respond to the past and to conjure the knowledge of this childhood. Memories control this section as they seem to be "just voice of another world" (12) and the poet finds himself as a "man with many memories who doesn't know what to do with them" (13). These personal reminiscences are also mixed with the memories of history, of war and peace, of the "swords of forgotten kings (which) rust slowly in the museums of our quilt" (14). Then the poet recollects his old father, his village, his daughter, and finally the rain, the cleanser of people and the earth. Looking at his mother's grave through the window, he not only tries to whirl back to the past, but also makes it appropriate to escape the burden of the real world. The poetic persona tries to identify himself with images from the familial past thus:

> Today I catch through the window
> the grave that is my mother's
> watch the old impulses in red and yellow
> chalked across of distant regains,
> as a member of some magician's audience
> watches a white rabbit
> flash out of the excited applause
> and vanish in air,...
> and the unidentifiable dead shadows
> strip the skin off my face,
> and from the body of the last green spring
> memory takes a road vague with the
> distance of loneliness and hurt
> away from the terrible glance of sky
> and its forest

where cranes bound into the surrounding silence,
and the clouds shift on the tears
of wounded pools of out living.

(*Relationship*, 12).

Now the poet comes out of his private tower and identifies himself with the majestic tradition that flows behind him. The careful withdrawal from the private past and the necessity to identify himself with the racial past is not only suggestive of a development but also a steadiness of the yearning to contain masses. A desire to involve himself in the affairs of current living makes his poetry more universal. And therefore the past, private or racial, remains a giver of joys and a redeemer of distresses. Mahapatra's concern with the past does not stem from a mere desire of idealizing it but from a desire of observing the progression of the present out of the past. This desire sanctions him an everlasting existence. The fleeting nature of time that creates a sense of loneliness in the poet helps him to relate himself to the three layers of time— the historical, the familial and the mythical. These three ideas of the past become for him a form of certainty in which one refines one's sense of identity:

What is real is this
wistful dreaming about that of the past,
and this my body, like a law of gravity
held forever, lost in insistent earth and fire.
And time, which slowly makes us
        forget out misery
for the emptiness in our own mouths,
falls upon my bowed head, and overripe
        melon or a vine,
its back of clay keeps an old habit going.

(*Waiting*, 13)

The third section of 'Relationship' is a harbinger of new life. And yet, he recollects the blood-red waters of the Daya River near Dhauli where Emperor Asoka turned from Chandasoka to Dharmasoka and began preaching the gospel of peace, Buddhism, and the memorandum of non-violence, peace. The poet recollects his rather few friends and the fluctuating gravels of their affection, relationships which are sometimes exaggerated by doubt, and even jealousy. Section four of the poem recapitulates the "theme-song of my life that burns my tongue" as well as the ancient love "of gold nose-rings / of the figures in the towering ruins / of stone, of regal lions, of their breasts /and armpits" (14). Section Four has a notable hymn to the Konark temple or the civilization frozen on its stones:

> And now, you, my ancient love of a hundred names,
> or rains and endless skies and morning mists,
> or wind-beaten evenings of owl-calls and of
> rice- harvests in December,
> my love of gold nose-rings and laughing earrings
> of towering ruins of stone panting in the dark,
> of loyal lions guarding the diamond novels of shrines
> of amber breasts and secret armpits ...
> (*Relationship*, 14)

Obeying his yearning to re-encounter the past, the narrator seeks light in vain from the millennium that stretches between modern and ancient Odisha. He declares:

> I know I can never come alive
> if I refuse to consecrate at the alter of my origins.
> (*Relationship*, 15)

Hence the poet is left with a sense of loneliness, bitterness, sorrowfulness—a consciousness of the emptiness of his own destiny. The section ends on an open note which is distinct from, but very much akin to, that of the end of the preceding section. The poet, hurt by the fear of ageing and death, and haunted by the shades of isolation, likes to redeem himself through a prayer which will allow him to link himself to the ancestors and to their lost generosities. He is finally up against the "emptiness of his own destiny". He is in a mood of prayer—a prayer to draw his body out and to reflect on the "earth's lost amplitudes". He also recalls the scene of the rain and the sunshine, the source of pure joy which have affected his susceptibility deeply.

In section five the poet lingers his glimpse into his dream world and his quest to probe into the 'miracle of living'. His country seems to him to be full of contradictions of the marvelous marriage pageants and also of lies and betrayals, a country in which the granite at Konark "binds the sun to a rhythm of desire" (15). The poet seems to echo Shakespeare that "We are such stuff / As dreams are made on, and our little life / Is rounded with a sleep." Mahapatra explores his imagining and also his state of inertia, and finally realizes that sleep "is a song that is heard from all sides continually" (21) unlike in Shakespeare's *The Tempest*, where sleep is a metaphor for dying. Section six also endures the poet's obsession with sleep and waking. The poet forestalls a storm and guesses that only a miracle can save mankind from this contemptable storm. Time moves on summarizing the nightmares of the Ganga Kings, who, having experienced their bloody battles and consequences of wars, now seem to be watching the ruins of their sequestered grief. Section seven seems to explore the poet's private world, his insomnia, his hallucinations, his quandaries in the midst of foreshadowing the invasion of the enemy into the defeated city—a city of his psyche where the armies of faith and doubt, innocence and guilt, of the past and present, clash at night only to make the poet aware of the dark night of his soul to make him realise that "martyrdom is not for those left alone in that no man's land". This message sounds rather like that of Jesus Christ or the Buddha, or even of Gandhiji on whom he writes rather long versions in his collection *Bare Face.*

In section eight the poet establishes a relationship between his own life and "this temple in ruins, in a blaze of sun". This is obviously a reference to the Sun Temple of Konark, one of the most magnificent pieces of sculpture and architecture in the world. The poet questions the lions standing near the—steps who are they waiting for ? The door, to understanding the essence of this great monument, lies through the knowledge of the mineral, vegetable, the animal world, through realizing the intensity of love and the deeper meaning of the earth. Mahapatra maintains:

> It is my own life
> that has cornered me beneath the stones
> of this temple in ruins, in a blaze of sun.
> Sun-lions, standing against the steps,
> whose return of life are you waiting for ?
> Whose roar to pulse through the veins
> of this first night of sleep ?...
> These things, hewn out of the darkness
> and of the light, of our ominous destination
> of the real and the imagined:
> the bronzed gazes of mermaids
> against the infinite blue of the sea,
> the night of the wild elephants pounding down
> in the undying sun,
> and the horned and the hooved,
> the 'gandharvas' and the demons,
> aren't these mere imitations we have made
> not having had enough of the sun's flight

across the purple hills of our guilt,
and the haunting down whose convex arcs of light
correspond to the dark abyss
of an absent dimension of the blood?

(Relationship, 27)

The next section attempts to unfold the "myth of happiness", the myth of "the wounded sun" encased in the Konark Sun Temple sculptures, the myth of "death" and also of those souls who survive the myth and are intertwined in the web of ideas, ideas which seem to stand like brooms on their shaky heads. In his poetic attempt to trace relationships, the poet envisages his dead grandfather, floating on the water, close to the burning pyre:

It is no use now if I try to wear
my grandfather's smile, disappearing
for an instant
in the midst of this myth; there are shadows
over my body, from the burning sun,
there are structures which blank the river
lacquered in red and fold.

(Relationship, 30)

In the tenth section, the poet recalls those moments when he stumbles out of his door to see the sage of troubled mien sitting under the peepul tree all alone, making him accept the silence which he feared. The poet celebrates an association with past:

For it seemed to be a time
when waters flow past without their purposes
when replicas of temples lie scattered everywhere
and thousands of fake huge eyes open wide in wood
inside them,

and bees become the lost witnesses
of an unknown honey before the storm.

(Relationship, 33)

The poet envisions the scene of Cuttack, where he was born and out of whose clay tiny images of goddesses were made year after, and the clay itself assume consecrated shapes. He tries to explore his own relationship with Cuttack and how he, as man and poet, becomes a willing progeny of that "mysterious inheritance":

Mysterious inheritance
in which roots stick out here and there
from the dung
of broken empires and of vanquished dynasties
and of ahinsa's whimpers;
for before I go to sleep
or go into the unknown in me
this house of blind windows built inside,
doesn't the fear it provides accelerate
our happiness ?

(Relationship, 34)

Ahimsa's whimpers are obviously an allusion to king Asoka and the Kalinga War, and the consequent *stupas* stand for universal peace. The poet stands among these ruins, waiting for the cry of hope, of a night bird and the voice of friends, creative artists, poets who, while being antagonized with the past, express their own creative rejoinder to their concentrated appeal. Mahapatra feels nostalgic among the ruins:

Now I stand among the ruins,
waiting for the cry of a night-bird.

(Relationship, 35)

In section 11 Mahapatra is basically concerned with what is "enduring" in the past and the relationship between past and present. What provokes and guides his journey now is not an observation of the of the umbilical link with the past but his disillusionment with the present. To the speaker the present is unsurprisingly personified in the nature and behaviour of his contemporaries and friends. The sense of a heroic achievement, the wonder of the involvement, and the familial commitment to his past, these three idioms form the very composite emotion suggested in this section 11, particularly in its conclusion.

In the twelfth and last section of *Relationship* the narrator makes two valedictory gestures. He says farewell to his old fearful guilty feeling that the past is something "beyond me that I cannot catch up". He then salutes the sculpted bodies of the dancing women on the temple stones, because it is to his contemplation of their dance that he is indebted for his new birth. And then he is enthused to speak to the prodigious beautiful figures in stone:

Is anything beyond me that I cannot catch up?
Tell me your names, dark daughters
Hold me to your spaces
In your dance is my elusive birth, my sleep
that swallows the green hills of the land
and the crows that quicken the sunlight in the veins
and the stone that watches my sadness fly in and out
of my deaths, a spiritless soul of memory.

(*Relationship,* 38)

An important and fascinating aspect of Mahapatra's *Relationship* shows his endeavor to connect not only the past with the present, but also to reconnoiter the involving links between one fine art and another, between statuette and poesy. In fact, it opens up an entirely new field of critical and esthetic appraisal of poetry. This is what is extraordinary about him. His mind's eye rises to far superior loftiness, and the substantial, pensive rhythms of his verse reproduce his greater concerns with time, death and the ambiguities of human life.

Among the Indian English poets, Jayanta Mahapatra is one of the few who speak of Indian domains with the pledge of an insider. For him, the Indian landscape establishes the purpose of Indians. In his poetry, one passes in the uncluttered world of stars, sky, wind, waves, rain, fields and trees. For him the Indian landscape is the detached location of his mental state, the segments of which get intimately mixed with the lyrical vocabulary of a human and humane faith. Even if his irony is healthy, yet skepticism is surprisingly absent in his poetry as it is accustomed by the temporary and inexplicable air of a landscape where past is intimately attached with the present and where myths and legends institute the folk tempo of a native susceptibility. India is too vast and diverse a notion to become so elaborate in poems. This is a place where a creative writer in an Indian language is relatively free. In his best poems, Mahapatra accomplishes the excellence of Indianness without special positions. To be an Indian, one has to evade deliberately trying to be an Indian. He need not give a performance like a snake-charmer or a mendicant. On the level of art the homegrown and the collective imagination must meet. This is what we find in the poetry of Jayanta Mahapatra. In "The Twenty-fifth Anniversary of a Republic" (1975) Mahapatra grotesquely describes the satirical status quo that has sneaked into his own country, affecting his countrymen. He apologetically writes:

This is a barren world that has been
prowling round my room, epidemics
in the poisoned air,

dusty streets stretching away like
   disgruntled socialists.

(A Father's Hours, 11)

And again,
The prostitutes are younger this year
at the police station they are careless
to give reasons for being what they are.
And the other women careful enough
not to show their years.

(A Father's Hours, 12)

Regarding his use of contemporary Indian degenerative situation as a subject of poetry, Bruce king gives an interesting remark:

Apparently surrealist techniques are used to explore through contradictions the inner world of the speaker and his relationship to his past, family, sexuality, nature and time, within a world where living is dying and the womb is seen leading to the tomb.[15]

In "The Lost Children of America" the poet catalogues the diverse planes of the jam-packed city Cuttack, comprehensive with diseases, corruptions, violence and wound:

Here
in the dusty malarial lanes
of Cuttack where years have slowly lost
their secrets...
corrupt politicians still
go on delivering their pre-election speeches
and on the high road above the
town's burning ground
from which gluttonous tan smoke floats up
in the breeze, smacking of scorched
merrow and doubt.

(Life Signs, 23)

Mahapatra's pervasive sense of despair reflected in his poetry might compel one to believe that his poetry is essentially pessimistic and tragic and that it could never transcend the overriding impact of cynicism. Mahapatra, a Christian living in a Hindu society, perhaps is more than a Hindu because of his insistence on destiny as all-powerful and supreme. It is perhaps because of his Christianity that he feels a sense of disaffection in a Hindu-dominated society. In order to escape from this sense of estrangement, he has perhaps consciously endeavored at portraying the rites, rituals and festivals of Odisha. His Christian self never makes a claim to be Christian, and because of this fundamental oxymoron, an ether of tension permeates everywhere. This pressure is patterned again by his relationship with the past. His Puri poems show the intensity of an individual's relation with his cultural heritage. In 'Dawn at Puri' he remembers his mother's last wish to be cremated at Puri:

> her last wish to be cremated
> twisting uncertainly like light on the shifting sand.
>
> (*A Rain of Rites*, 28)

> Even in Puri
> when the world,
> silent again
> for a moment,
> begins to speak again,
> I long for Puri.
>
> (*Sky without Sky*, XIX)

A legend says that Dharma, the 12-year-old son of Bisu Maharana, after putting the crown slab of the Sun

Temple, committed suicide to protect the respect, the dignity of the 1,200 masons. Mahapatra forgets his personal sense of loss in the method of ageing when he compares it with the loss grafted in the veins of Odia tradition; idiosyncratic feelings seem less arduous before an unbiased pain of nationalism:

> I must carry the stone I found
> in the late afternoon light
> let me not think of myself only,
> and my pain which processes
> these last breaths of my life.
> Konark, black in sleep,
> cold bacon of my silent land,
> messenger of death.
> Here the little boy in a dream
> waved to the man once
> and death hung its peace;
> an indifferent time of stone
> marks the burnt out funeral pyre
> and the sun rise
> that journeys again and again
> to call this grief of man
> its own.

> *(Waiting,* 22)

It is evident that Mahapatra, in the development of reconnoitering his roots, falls back on the deposits of the racial past and holds these very profoundly so much so that the burden of the self gets interpreted by the positive phantasmagoria of the place. Falling back on the past, both familial and cultural, revitalizing the spirits of innocence embedded in the rituals and myths, he not only celebrates his sense of the place but also advocates for the willingness to live by:

...Alone again
with time to question myself
I begin with the kind things
I must say to others
because of my fear,
with the lineament of acceptance
spread over my wounded past's breast,
knowing that the pigeons of my town
must fly and perch on the unspoken sadness
of the bronze statue
decapitated once in sudden redness.

(Dispossessed Nests, 35)

He is at once upset to realize the callousness of people in the relapsed world for:

Here the last house in the city
are simply smiling into the darkness.
Now a man knows only two ways
for dealing with a stray woman:
he rapes her
and kills her.

(Dispossessed Nests, 33)

He painfully tries to sympathize with the people who wish to disown the sense of history:

The weariness of the ages festers
into hard knots of meanness here and there
The taste that comes of our leaders
shirking the questions of people's existence,
The shame of travellers who have lost their ways
in India.
The cold stairs down to the water
their breathing rasping hoarsely in
the winter mist
The tall dark mountains burying their faces

in the false snow to stifle their laughter
The river wailing with the strange choice of the lost
riding on until all it felt
was the darkness and the rush of
stranger seas.

*(Dispossessed Nests, 34)*

The poet rather is disturbed to encounter a besmirched India for he has always loved a myth-ridden, divine, nonviolent India:

The country urges us to seek
the stars at night
too fill as we are of mystic battles, angry gods
and the heroism of Hanuman. Upon these
distant pinpoints of light
we night reconstruct
some other world, dinging memory, journeying
no more. No more. Ah love, we had read so much
about you, about freedom. Was everything you did,
Gandhiji, only an act you put on for Posterity ?
With India, our India, barely, worth raping ?

*(Dispossessed Nests, 34)*

Yet he identifies himself with this country with a rich artistic heritage:

I know I have been in love with the world
a little too much, taken my own place
for granted and become the secret landscape
like the redeeming monument of a Gandhi,
in the India of my illusive glass.

*(Dispossessed Nests, 35)*

His "wounded past's breast" is wounded to see the dishonesty in politics in the present state:

The hail of glass and plaster
looks on at his humility

as the calendar hatches India's history
a lifeless story
chewed on by the vultures of a
country's leaders.

*(Dispossessed Nests, 30)*

Then again comes the character of the poet when he says:

We never take our lives seriously
or perhaps we don't let ourselves get carried away.

*(Dispossessed Nests, 31)*

The 'Khalistan Issue' even comes to the pen of the poet:

...the lonely woman
standing in the queue for her sustenance
allowance (her husband shot dead by
terrorists last month)
a voice which the roar
of the Ministers' jet cuts short.

*(Dispossessed Nests, 24)*

Then again a shift of theme, again the recollection of father:

And the old man whom I call father
slowly opens his mouth to swallow
the spoonful of glucose being fed to him.
I have been watching him lie in his bed
for over two years now.

*(Dispossessed Nests, 24)*

Then the poet writes in the memory of Leela, a girl who died in Bhopal gas tragedy:

The eyes are deep and hard in Leela's sockets.
And the face looks peaceful in death.
That's what they say, the onlookers.
What would Leela have said
had she grown up to her father's age ?

*(Dispossessed Nests, 41)*

John Oliver Perry's views about the *Dispossessed Nests* are noteworthy is this context:

> *Dispossessed Nests* represents a departure. Perhaps, if the differences mark a trend, there is a development towards increased social relevance and away from tracing the inner pains of culturally, geographically and existentially imposed constraints on unwilled, indistinct personal desires. Never callous or complacent about his national and cultural tensions, Mahapatra here seems to accept the special function of poets in so-called transitional or developing societies, to help bridge the gap between traditional and modern, urban and rural, privileged and poor.[16]

When in the peripheral world, the poet meets an elaborate world, changed and shifting beyond appreciation, he discovers the changes taking place within him originated by the crusade of time:

> I am that stranger now
> my mirror holds to me;
> the moment's silence
> hardly moves across the glass,
> I pity myself in another's guise.
>
> (*Life Sign*, 36)

The poet distinguishes the meaning of physical strength and his fear of death somewhere, when he is no longer young. No longer can he recapture his own youth which became a thing of the past:

> And no one's back here, no one
> I can recognize, and from my side
> I see nothing. Years have passed
> since I sat with you, watching

the sky grow lovelier with cloudlessness
waiting for your body to make it lived in.

*(Life Sign, 36)*

Words flow rhythmically, merging sound and image,
always harnessed in by a landscape where time has stood
in stagnant stillness. In 'River' Mahapatra hints:

This river
haunted and grave
by the last cries of men
trying to reach
the opposite share.
Open mouthed
like the water,
memory.
Across the flat priestly darkness
an eagle appears
flapping greyly
and it sounds
like the weary thump
of my dead grandfather's heart..."

*(Life Signs, 37)*

In this volume, a persuasive way of life is
counterbalanced by a private image of the poet. Daniel Mc.
Bride gives his opinion about *Life Signs* thus:

The mood here is consistently philosophical as
Mahapatra brings out the void between
perceiver and perceived, poet and reader, across
which a glittering array of poetic experiences
form after images the veiled epiphanic moments
of age that in denying any reassuring meaning
must deny the very possibilities of human
hope.[17]

The poems deal with themes collectively accessible,

like the ocean, but at the same time certain specifics like Chandipur-on-sea are emphasized. The sea symbolizes what is ancient, traditional, altering, yet the same. The sea "spits out the gauze wings of shells along the beach" ;(*Life Sins*, p. 10) spits out what is 'lost' or is slowly crumbling. Breaking himself out of the spell of the imprisoned air, he turns to his people:

Who can tell...

of smells paralysed throughout the centuries of deltas

hard and white that stretched once to lure the feet of women bidding their men goodbye ?

(*Life Signs*, 18)

There was a time around the first century A.D. in Orissa when her merchants used to carry on maritime trade dealing in spices across the seas to Java, Sumatra and Bali and their women came to the seashore to see them off — it retains its charm for its archetypal sexual pattern embedded in the metaphor "deltas hard and white" (20) around which the question is woven: the pain at separation. In the next line one finds Mahapatra at his workshop of poetry defining the landscapes, physical and intellectual, of the women of his land, of the "salt and light" (20) that their "dark and provocative eyes" appreciate while their "shoulders are dropping like lotuses in the noonday sun" (20). With the close of the first paragraph of the poem is the "drooping" of a celebrated chapter of history. The beginning of another paragraph of the same poem opens up another episode of history, that is our time which the poet looks upon as a question mark. Again the riddle of the words, "who are you / occupant of the silent sigh of the conch?" (25) becomes momentous when one knows that these women bidding their men goodbye blew a conch as a propitious sign. Thus the question evokes as much an ancient aura as a disrespect of present, the question being set on the threshold of two different times, two different traditions of life. Those grounds seem to be only a reminiscence now, the memory which redeems the poet's brooding heart. In this poem the poet's silence breaks like a face beneath, his dreams in front of his ancestors. Again, the sad tales about his people who are poor, yet they cannot forget their old age faith in their gods, the inaccessible gods of thorny words, mute and silent, impenetrable to a massive nationwide grief and the corrupted politicians are other subjects of the poetry of Mahapatra. A political tone and religious theme are delicately brought into a harmony, in the poem "A Country". He writes:

> I look at their faces and their eyes are
> dead as stone;
> He is my world, and it makes the dream
> as a child.

*(Life Signs, 26)*

In 'Grandfather', Mahapatra records the 1866 famine of Odisha, a picture of which one can find in explanation in the Odia novel *Haa Anna* by Kanhu Charan Mohanty. 'Grandfather', is the most intense confessional poem of Mahapatra. Though the poem is about the edifice of a civilization during 'the ancestors, yet the poet himself with his embarrassment , with the burden of a Hindu profile of lineage on his conscience, anchors at the centre of the poem. Written against a shocking and dark chapter of history, "the yellowed diary's notes" of his grandfather, "whispering in vernacular" could be the yellowed pages of his nation's history. The use of the word "vernacular" postulates a history that is his own, his people's. Then follows the portrayal of the famine-stricken land and the famine-stricken mental make-up of her victims:

No uneasy stir of cloud
darkened the white skies of your day; the silence
of dust gazed in the long afternoon sun, ruling
the cracked fallow earth, ate into the
laughter of your flesh.
For you it was the hardest question of all
Dead, empty trees stood by the dragging against your
sleep. You thought of the way the jackals moved, to move.

*(Life Signs,* 23)

The poet understands his grandfather's moral feebleness and hence he is compassionate with him:

What Hindu world so ancient and true
for you to hold

*(Life Sign,* 23)

"Grandfather" is not a case of amnesia but the memory of trailing of a vibrant past. He and his son sit down to know:

What it was to be, against dying
to know the dignity
that has to be earned dangerously.

*(Life Signs,* 24)

In 'The Vase' the poet advances a similar view of his getting colder and older by years. Metaphorically, he introduces the change that has gone into his body:

The tree trembles in the wind
the house where we once made love
now weakens at the knees. And all the time
that gathered into these moments
fills the grave of the vast vase with dust.

*(Life Signs,* 37)

All these years the poet has professed modesty to face death. He is sure that neither degeneration nor death can snatch away man's most appreciated custody, 'memory'.

Even in becoming extinct the poet likes to commemorate the disjointed moments of life:

Come December
Until I discover sad remnants of wind
left behind at the cross-roads of life:

(*The False Start*, 36)

"Measuring Death" reveals death's revulsion and its secret bliss for being alive. Man's indomitable pursuit for light takes him to the empire of obscurity with death and all its unconceivable revulsions:

Again and again you look to the light
hoping it would somehow find your kingdom
but there beyond is the cold bank of darkness
where every man stands alone, for
himself.

(*The False Start*, 74)

The poet tries to estimate death's ubiquity through the allegory of sunlight:

Like the great sunlight inside the leaf
this death is there, growing out
from under the backbones
lying in the midst of our wreckage.

(*The False Start*, 76)

The key sentence in *The False Start* occurs in the poem "Time Drawing In" where the poet feels the fragility of his life again. It also rationalizes Mahapatra's insolence that most of us have taken a false start in our lives, and need to be called back to the opening points to begin the challenge of life once again, so that we may do well in not only evading the feebleness, but also in having the moral courage to resist society's "taunting laughter that fills the hollow years" (34). Time that "flutters like a prayer flag", as Mahapatra puts it in a poem titled "Today" is perhaps the only complex bystander and observer to our measured but sturdy loss of its inculpability. The central theme of his poetry is that our feebleness of the past and their empathetic mood can alone make us cognizant of as to how much dishonest our life's start has been. The past may pollinate us again with a energizing liveliness to live a life with scarcer feebleness, or even rarer blunders. Regarding the landscapes that Mahapatra takes up in *The False Start* Syed C. Harrex writes, "*The False Start*, is of remarkable consistency of tone, preoccupation, theme, image, vocabulary .... This landscape is a kind of meeting place for elementalist and transcendentalist concerns.[18]

Mahapatra's poems on Odisha vis-à-vis its historical and cultural past, create a defense mechanism that secures the poet against the development which insulates him and generates a disconcerted fear of death. Relapsing into the private past and the past of his own place, he defies his elusion from the complications of the present. But this escapist strategy should not be taken into consideration because it helps him to introduce a rapport with the past, and instantaneously to make the present eloquent. Realization of the unavoidability of death forces him to discover for himself a place which would persist to be untouched by the forces of death. He scrupulously believes that a nation never dies nor does its ethos, a place never fades away; both tolerate transformation and both integrate crusade through changes. It is indeed because of this realization that he discharges from his own microcosmic persona and it comprises the macrocosmic and unbiased world for him.

Norman Simms reasons that Mahapatra's poetry generates three inscapes. The first inscape tries to show the resistance between the two worlds of institution and modernism. The second inscape is the development of creative writing itself.

> The third inscape is the one that is created by Mahapatra's writing: by the actual poems, to be sure, but also by the process itself, which engages him in a self-conscious ritual of discovery when the self that emerges is perceived as a 'stranger', yet also by the consequences of his decision to be a poet, which means, first to be aware of editors, general readers and critics, that is to find a new set of references developing around him, a new awareness of sensible listeners, a sense of resonance of his own voice that could not exist unless he were a poet.[19]

Myths polish his mind's eye and reinforce his suppression with a people who use them with comprehensive faith, contribution.

In the twentieth century the independent theory of time has acquired preference due to Bergson's philosophy of existentialism. As common human beings, we are conscious of time, of the sequence of events, of intervals of time. Mahapatra incorporates the above concepts of time into his poetry in various forms, and at the same time acquaints us with some of his significant notions of time. For him, time carries a sense of urgency, a feeling of helplessness at the thought of not being able to discharge from the immediate response which possesses him and perhaps becomes a case of estimation, bring it with a realization of the final trial of life. There is an amalgamation of spiritual and chronological experiences of time—time as it exists in peripheral truth and as the poet feels it in relation to the events of his life. He views his personal time as all time, as an interminable stretch, but finds its standing in its transporting maturity to human life; he looks upon the cyclical fluctuations in nature and connects them with the method of ageing in human beings. He does not discard old age and death as raw knowledges of human life. He accepts them with an apathetic defiance and wisdom. It is through time that man learns and practices life. His notion of writing poetry is similar to somewhat with that of T S Eliot. In an interview with Norman Simms he gives emphasis on depersonalization, reminding us of the Theory of Impersonality:

Life is painful, the process of writing center of yourself and I suppose you cannot do this if you don't give up your own self.[20]

Poetry is a kind of self-discovery, introspection for the poet. Mahapatra looks for the meaning of life, for the explanation of the ambiguities of life, and seeks to accomplish a certain vision of life in his poetry. His poetry divulges his space between self and the habit that nurtures the self. If in his early poetry, the past occurred as a dream world of love and involvement, joy and hope, in his later poetry the past is the remnant of the basic motive behind his cultural consciousness and racial awareness. It is the familiarity with the past that makes one's life evocative and germane. The poet's standing condenses to a commoner when he writes:

There is a past which moves over
the magic slopes and hamlets of the mind
whose breath measures the purpose of our lives.

(*The False Start*, 44)

Mahapatra's *Temple* is a volume of a different palate. Here he pays a tribute to Maa Durga, the ideal goddess of Bengal or Odisha. In this volume, Maa Durga has two aspects: saber-toothed Kali with a necklace of skulls, and the softly beautiful moon goddess *Chandni* or some other more fostering *devi*. Also in the *Temple* 'feminine principle' is identified as "the divine force which emerges in times of need", epitomized by *Shakti* and associated with Brahminic definitive perception, because in Hindu mythology they are one and the same. John Oliver Perry writes:

> The multiforme feminine being felt so devastatingly in Mahapatra's poetic imagination are comprehensible not only as figures from mythic worlds, Hindu or otherwise; they also constitute complex symbols for an alternative self.[21]

They may be treated as disturbed predictions into another being of the powerfully differed personal needs that are discovered in this poetry of sensitive edge. As Mahapatra explains in his autobiography, "I wanted so frantically to build a bond of love." At last in *Temple* he has initiated a condition in which that longing can be persuasively articulated. Remorsefully and timidly and with continued ambiguity and inconspicuousness, he projects his frantic needs and proud autonomy into a faintly apparent character found in a newspaper note, a poor and lonely 80 years old suicide, Chelammal. By identifying with Chelammal's misery and refabricating her perception, 'Jayanta', as he calls himself in the poem, chooses prognosis as a suitable means to deal with his characteristically unhappy and troubled feelings. The conditions of the news story and the poet's narrative make Chelammal's sufferings, "the plight of Indian women" (*Temple*, 51). In "Waiting" a poem of 44 lyrics, the poet deals with Vedic themes, there are frequent references to death and leprous skin. The scientist in Mahapatra meets the Vedic Agni as the Divine

Will-Force, Indra as Mind Power, Vayu as Life Energy, Varuna and Mitra as Truth working in the human mind, the Cows as the Rays of Truth— consciousness, Dawn as the power to wake us to the revelation of Truth and Surya as Truth-consciousness itself. In the *Burden of Waves and Fruit*, the poet deals with old age and death. Old age has come to him like a 'weary night bird' like an ashen owl on a branch of his breath. In an interview with *The Indian Express* he has said: "I have been working hard somehow feeling that I don't have much time left. The morbid streak you find in my poetry is also there within me. The idea of death has always been with me."[22] Perhaps this death-consciousness, this self-doubt makes him fall back on the past. It is the awareness into his ageing that has kept him from disappearing into the dark pit of his freezing self. His self has come to live in terms with his body, with an intemperance:

'a careless memory inhibits my walk'.

(*Burden of Waves and Fruit*, 17)

In *A Father's Hours*, Mahapatra finds a likelihood of an juncture of time with the timeless, an uncommon healing by the physicality of the flesh. The poet is in doubt, can past redeem us from humiliation and distress? Perhaps it can.

Is the past
that rises from the ground
to swallow us up?
Does it suffice
to protect us from our shame?

(*A Father's Hours*, 17)

Mahapatra's turning back to the place of his birth and childhood has become a desire that keeps him away from the fear of being anonymous in this swarming cosmos. The vanished moments come back to the poet in order to rejuvenate his present with a sense of curiosity and amazement—curiosity because of the interruption of the past into the present, amazement because of the fact that the present would dissolve into the past. In the recollection of his lost love he sings:

> It is November and I can ask for more,
> because I do not know you even in memory,
> and my need touches new hands,
> but the bells ring,
> in your faraway summer heart
> under your sleeping breasts,
> perhaps to begin a little dance of time
> that's caught with my few unspoken words
> as they bow their heads over your
> awakening.
>
> (*Burden of Waves and Fruit*, 34)

Regarding the transitory nature of time, Mahapatra writes:

> The country's storm
> has died down. My hands kiss rock,
> seek the meek combs of rust on the stone.
> And the blood-red sun is simply the mask of a child
> who dances away for us, evening after evening.
>
> (*Burden of Waves and Fruit*, 19)

This sudden realization makes the poet nostalgic:

> This is the time when the fruit of my life
> seems humble and tender against the dark banyan
> when the season comes alive with memories
> of earlier years.
>
> (*Burden of Waves and Fruit*, 27)

Here again, as it is typical of Mahapatra, he perambulates between personal and the cultural history of

Odisha. In "Shapes by the Daya" he writes an elegy for the thousands of Odias who were slaughtered by the armies of emperor Asoka on the banks of river Daya:

> Time rests its terrible quiet on the river.
> And the wind blows everywhere, words dance
> like the ghastly remains of long-dead men
> by the light of a cold moon,
> in these skies
> as though they were a fearful place to be named in.
>
> (*Burden of Waves and Fruit*, 21)

Always these "dead things loom larger with every hour that goes" (53). The preparedness to hurry homeward remains essential to Mahapatra's vision of being a homebound pilgrim. In a conversation with Norman Simms he talks about his home:

> I remember my father telling the stories when lie came home from his tours; my mother, my younger brother and I lived in a house which was surrounded by tall deodars, and I still have the feeling of evil shapes lurking in those trees through the nights. He liked shooting too (hunting, I mean) but we never shot much, and I don't like it".[23]

Whether it is remembrance of home or the inmates of home, Mahapatra falls back on them to revitalize his strength to antagonize the indispensable realities of life. And it is through recollection—both familial and historical—that he attains comfort, security, redemption. In an article titled "Song of the Past : An Interpretation of the Poetry of Jayanta Mahapatra", G. Sundari and K.S. Ramamurti write:

> An acute preoccupation with the past and the problem of coming to terms with it seem to be the dominant motifs which inform the poetry

of Jayanta Mahapatra and control all its varying moods. His poetry unravels a fabric of the past, woven with a few relevant historical details of the land of Orissa and its 'rains everywhere/ holding dim interiors of myth' and the rites and rituals centred on the three temples at Bhubaneswar, Puri and Konark symbolizing a hoary tradition of which he is an inheritor. This concern with the past is the natural consequence of an awareness of the passage of time. [24]

Mahapatra's keen response to the passage of time is significant in some of his poems like "The Morning", "Night Fall", "Afternoons", "Dusk", "Another Evening", "The Day", "A Saturday Afternoon". The seasonal variations are found in such poems as "A Rain", "Summer", "Indian Summer Poem", "The Earth of July" and in some poems of his collection of poems titled *Shadow Space* (1997). To interpret the poetry of Mahapatra from the point of view of his approach towards the past and the tradition of the land of Odisha is an inquisitive search for any researcher. About his Odisha poems, K. Ayyappa Panikar writes:

Mahapatra's Indian quality is perhaps most keenly felt in his poems about Orissa. He sounds more authentic when he' writes about Orissa than about India as a whole. This has considerably enhanced the intrinsic power of his poems derived largely from the local detail raised to universal significance. [25]

"Orissa Landscapes", "Evening in an Orissa Village", "The Oriya Poems", "Down at Puri", etc., are Odia sensibilities poems. In Mahapatra's best works, the language is English, but the sensibility is certainly Odia. In his volume of poems, *Shadow Space* (1997) he begins by writing about the ancestral past of Odisha, and how far it has put an impression upon our present. And above all, reminiscence of the bygone days of every man is the chief subject here. In the first poem "Living in Orissa", he gives a picture of Odisha at present, a present that has perhaps cut off its relationship with indigenous Odisha:

> To live here
> antlered in sickness and disease
> in the past of uncomprehended totems,
> and the split blood of ancestors
> one would wear like an amulet.
> ... Only shadows shift now.
> They have the eyes of defeated spirits.
> The old eyes.
>
> (*Shadow Space*, 11)

The poet feels time, the greatest healer, does no more answer man's questions:

> Again the fields of man are rugged with fear.
> And the breast of young girls
> do not rise and fall with their own breathing.
> And when a shudder passes through
> the thin body of the wing
> that sees so much, we are prepared
> to tolerate our unhappiness with God.
> Time answers impassively once again,
> here above the tomb of someone unknown,
> in the sombre fabric of crows' flight.
> And silence condemns, left behind
> by the great net of time's vendetta.
>
> (*Shadow Space*, 12)

Hence he wishes to go back to a past even if it were fragmented; and seems unredeemable:

Yet your own past is too large
for you to talk sensibly about it.
Held fast in the embrace of one's own history
your silence is a part of that truth
which leaves you older than before.

(*Shadow Space*, 14)

And in some of the poems, Mahapatra recollects the perilous World Wars, writes about the pointlessness of war:

Writing my poems again,
what do I remember of faith and past hopes ? Mine
was the generation that paid homage to Gandhi and
Tagore, saw in my mother the stare of Dostoyevsky's
Grand Inquisitor. It was the end of the War,
the beginning of the curse of beggardom.

(*Shadow Space*, 16)

In yet another poem, "Japan-II", he writes about the pity of Second World War, encounters a mother and her child who had lost everything in the war:

Which city are you from" ? I asked.
"Tokyo ? Or Nagasaki" ?
But only a hint of a smile came back in reply.
A cricket cried out stupidly from the bare maples.
The strident engines of stars echoed in the night.

(*Shadow Space*, 53)

And in "Aftermath" he writes about the Gulf War, and the misfortunes thereof. Mahapatra sounds rather cynical about the regenerating power of the past

It's the root we need, the drums that talk
the musk breath of earth that must echo
the speechless word of a chained vanity, a hold
to bless the past that doesn't seem real anymore.

(*Shadow Space*, 21)

His soul gets restless to bear this burden of living:

> If the world weeps, are you moved ?
> Will it show you where to go ?
> Does the world grow according to its own needs ?
> Pity is only felt for one
> whose eyes are blind to the ways of another.
> With those eyes
> I cannot walk barefoot here.
>
> *(Shadow Space,* 23)

Hence the poet is led to the world of recollection, recollection of his familial past where suffering was the way of life:

> My father took four long years to die,
> lying on the edge of his pus-filled bed sores.
> My mother looked at him and took her pills
> and pretended illness ; it was only
> the justification of her own life.
> Death is never that simple.
> Both knew that they were lying;
> they did not turn their eyes away.
>
> *(Shadow Space,* 24)

Again, the pangs of death. The idea of death that "seems so necessary here/for the clam lassitude/that follows a violent disturbance" (35). Death disrupts the poet so that "standing at the grave of my father I too/deny myself a bit of my life" (42). "Shadows" is a poem in this collection where the poet considers the past as a shadow that has abandoned him:

> Shadows can never open their mouths.
> They don't talk politics. Or love.
> Do I have a shadow I have lived in ?
> Do I have one which regards me ...
> I think my shadow ruined me a long time ago.
>
> *(Shadow Space,* 38)

But the letdown is that, there is no way to get distanced
from the shadow:

How do I come out of the shadows,
those that want to be with me,
surrounding my face like mask,
when I know I am doing the right thing
for the wrong reasons ?

(*Shadow Space*, 38)

In another poem "Enterprise" he wants to get hold
of the past so that memory will always appear anew,
innovative:

Beyond the trees, an endless night
whose past pins me to the earth ; and I
wanting the past not to be the past,
and the sense of an empty hand still
    pressed down
over the photograph of an impossible exultation.

(*Shadow Space*, 44)

Yet the poet never wants to be free from history, the
history of humankind:

Why wait to be free of history
when you are now in it ?
Secrets will begin to speak
ashes soak in the rivers.
And the streets
go on enjoying their dead—
either in Jerusalem
or in Delhi or distant Nicaragua.

(*Shadow Space*, 66)

Here also, recollection acts as a mode of redemption
for the poet:

... I don't want to read Plato.
Or Nehru's glimpses of India, for that matter.

The house I live in is calm. The few, silent,
desperate words I've learned these past
years have trapped my soul.

(Shadow Space, 57)

"A Day in the Marburg on-the-Lahn" is a poem when
he laments over the death of poet A. K. Ramanujan
recollecting their days of togetherness in Germany:

I remember so many things you said, sitting there,
about Chicago where you had been living for years
and were on your way back to from Israel.
How far away, I wondered, those places and my own
homeland that was indeterminate, a possibility
called India, at that moment which was not past,
not future.

(Shadow Space, 47)

To cherish Ramanujan's memoirs, he fondly preserves
his gift:

I have wanted to tell you that I have not yet
opened the bottle of champagne you brought me.
It's four years now. The pen gets heavier each day
But not the sight of your frail figure
as you crossed a cobbled Marburg street
with the abundant gentleness on your face.

(Shadow Space, 48)

Thus in almost all the poems, memory is the key
theme, the personal memory expressed in a rather
impersonal way:

When you are safely distant from living,
you can worship the murdered Gandhi.
You can speak about
the world you were born in ...

(Shadow Space, 65)

*Bare Face* is the poetry collection of Mahapatra in

which memory, again, works as a mode of redemption. Here the poet takes up violence, darkness, death as recurrent themes. The social, cultural, familial past and his helplessness against the misery, hunger and poverty of his country are the repeated leitmotifs. The freedom struggle of India is painted by the poet in the Gandhi poems. In an interview, Mahapatra had said that he was working on a long poem on Gandhiji, and may be the second part of the volume *Bare Face* is the outcome. Now the high and dry poet pitiably contemplates on the plight of his country, dirges for the present state of affairs, and his concern for history, for the past glory of India come out with affluence and fluidity. But now he sometimes seems to have started accepting life as it is, trying to drive out the obscurity from his heart, heading towards precision, culmination. In the poem "Collaboration", familial past, the father image comes out again.

> The mango tree my father and I planted
> drifts blindly along the monsoon rain,
> the air underneath its branches
> in deep, cold and clear.
> His dead face is poised vaguely somewhere
> is the soft talk in the corridors
> of my childhood I haven't left behind.
> Dogs bark in this lost hour of mine.
> We were so close to each other that time.
>
> *(Bare Face,* 15)

> Yet the poet doubts the tradition of the past:
> How I have waited, shaped by memory,
> these many years without knowing exactly why.
> Does childhood spread out all the way
> from the hills of innocence to the horizon of the sea ?
>
> *(Bare Face,* 18)

The mother of the poet has been a poetic personae for him, now he understands how she has grieved throughout her life for the sake of love and writes in "The Woman who Wanted to be Loved":

Seasons pass, and she becomes stone.
Sighs of mango blossoms bring in
the scents summer scentless around the bone. Love can break and still keep its promise.
It can borrow a dawn and haunt it through time.

(*Bare Face*, 28)

In a recent poem "After the Death of a Friend", the similar tone reappears:

Grief, and more grief, taking us nowhere.
My mother is wearing a discolored dress
and she's been dead for years now.
Noises of the play-acting buffoonery of children
harassing a madman in the street reach me.

(*Hesitant Light*, 9)

In "Sometimes", the poet writes on the relevance of Mahatma Gandhi today:

Even the headless torso of Gandhi
in the city square can speak.
Like truth, unsaid most of the time,
yet almost said.

(*Bare Face*, 29)

Even if the poet has a sense of belongingness to the present, he is agonized because of the fleeting nature of time and confesses, "the last hours of memory hold only darkness" (p.20) because "Time is unreal like a paper star that rises out of sight and away" (p.20). But again, being scared of the present the poet takes recluse in the past and writes in 'The Taste of Sunlight':

Even my old widowed mother looks at me
and knows I fear the thought of love,
and my face shapes the thought,
of what one has only been taught to do,
terrified as I am
by the gentleness of sunlight upon my cheek.

(*Bare Face*, 33)

In the poem "Freedom" the poet sounds ironic about the present state of affairs in the Indian political scenario, the poem tries to make us aware of the value of freedom:

Here, old widows and dying men
cherish their freedom,
bowing time after time in obstinate prayers .
... In order for me not to lose face,
it is necessary for me to be alone.
Not to meet the woman and her child
in that remote village in the hills
who never had even a little rice
for their one daily meal these fifty years.
And not to see that uncaught, blooded light
of sunsets cling to the tall white columns
of Parliament House.

(*Bare Face*, 34)

In poems like "The Tame Ending" and "Brothers", Mahapatra uses beautiful images to designate the birth of a poem, or about the philosophy behind Indian rites and rituals:

The poem is like a lost child wailing
near a lamp post, uncomforted by the coin
thrust into its fist by a passerby.

(*Bare Face*, 39)

And,
Our rites have become burdens

given to us like curses upon our souls,
and hope has become God, difficult to see.

                                    (*Bare Face*, 40-41)

Even sometimes the poet desires to enter the cocoon of the world of poetry being isolated. In "Lines of My Poem" he writes in utter defeat:

Poem, my mother, how
pain has made you cross
the divide between past and future.
You are the cocoon
of my broken soul.

Since "It is hard here to live a number of lives" (48), the poet is wounded to face life after an Australian missionary and his two young sons were burnt alive in Odisha on the night of January 22nd, 1999, and writes an elegy for them, "Progress". The poem "Prologue" is written on 'the bodiless God of Puri' (55), as such, making us yet more sentient of the cultural heritage of Odisha. Section IV of "Requiem" is about the Salt Satyagraha in India in 1930. The poet suffers to see us postmoderns running away from history:

Today, where history is,
it is as if the events were never real.
Our childhood hours drift away,
looking for nowhere.

                                    (*Bare Face*, 60)

Hence, in absolute defeat, with a sense of loss, agony, with the idea of an uncertain future, Mahapatra concludes:

Now I live on, healthy, wise,
without a past
with an uncertain future.

                                    (*Bare Face*, 68)

Here, the poetic personae epitomizes the modern

man. He is the prototype of the men of our cohort. In many of his autobiographical accounts, articulated in his short prose pieces and interviews, Mahapatra has recurrently and candidly said that when he started writing poetry, his knowledge of poetry did not go beyond a few poems of Wordsworth, Keats and Shelley, prescribed in the school syllabus. Jayanta Mahapatra's search for his roots developed an intense poetic passion in him that motivates him often to attain a continued creative level, although he feels unsatisfied because, "no one seems to need"…"my answer", and second, because he has doubts that the "sleepless life" he "walks on leads nowhere". Anyway, his philosophical gravity of poetic density has preordained for him adapting ancient Hindu strategies with modern techniques, or perhaps amending contemporary English poetic applications with local traditional strategies. Reader response is the need of the hour to comprehend Mahapatra. Out of the apparent representation of Indian cultural landscape, symbolism and myth, of moveable modernists' operational forms and premeditated uncertainties, and of a vague, inquisitively distanced, yet all-encompassing ability to speak, the most bewildering entity in Mahapatra is the arrangement of a poetic-self despite all the ostensible efforts at individual liberty.

One can safely say that Mahapatra takes up the past—familial, cultural, historical—to discover his own identity in a callous world of detached men. Memory helps him to realize his own worth, to find solace away from the burdens of the present. Vilas Sarang asserts that "Mahapatra's poetry seems to point towards the direction that Indian English poetry will take most fruitfully."[26] This critical approbation that Sarang accords to the poetry of Mahapatra is not shocking, considering the fact that despite the deceptively 'unparaphrasable' nature of his poetry, Mahapatra continues to be read and discussed, both in India and abroad, and his influence on the younger poets is distinctly perceptible. Obscurity is his weakness and strength, both, to make him discrete and different.

I would conclude my critical discourse by quoting the bard himself from his recent poetry collection, *Sky without Sky: The Puri Poems*, published by Poetrywalla in 2018.

" I painfully realize that the poetry I've written (and much has been published in the last fifty years) has been restricted perhaps to the apparently colloquial narrative poem, which meditates on not so much of reality, but struggle to go deep into the nothingness that surrounds us in this world of ours. I have suffered this, but have truly gone nowhere. Talking about what this poetry reveals is difficult; chaos in the outside world has always been a challenge, but seems to be relevant to the poetry I've done.

Many of my first poems were thematically on the temple town of Puri, which has been the lifeline of the Odia people for centuries. It has been a subject poets in Odisha have never been able to resist. For all of us, I'd say.

Puri remains a difficult question for all time and demands a long answer. It's not for me to comment if the poems in this slim volume have any answers in the poems' solitudes. Suffice it to say that it is all part of the journey I began years and years ago."

# WORKS CITED

## PRIMARY SOURCES

### *Poetry in English*
*Close the Sky*, *Ten by Ten*, Calcutta. Dialogue Publications, 1971
*Svayamvara and Other Poems*, Calcutta. Writers Workshop, 1971
*A Father's Hours*, Calcutta. United Writers, 1976.
*A Rain of Rites*, Athens. University of Georgia Press, USA, 1976
*Waiting*, New Delhi. Samkaleen Prakashan, 1979
*The False Start*, Bombay. Clearing House, 1980
*Relationship*, Greenfield. Greenfield Review Press, New York., USA, 1980
*Life Signs*, New Delhi. Oxford University Press, 1983
*Dispossessed Nests*, Delhi/Jaipur. Nirala Publications, 1986
*Selected Poems*, New Delhi. Oxford University Press, 1987
*Burden of Waves and Fruit*, Washington, DC. Three Continents Press, USA, 1988
*Temple*, Sydney/Mundelstrup/Coventry. Dangaroo Press, 1989
*A Whiteness of Bone*, New Delhi. Viking Penguin, 1992
*The Best of Jayanta Mahapatra*, Kozhikode. Bodhi Publications, Kerala, 1995
*Shadow Space*, Kottayam. D.C.Books, Kerala, 1997
*Bare Face*, Kottayam. D.C.Books, Kerala, 2000
*Random Descent*, Bhubaneswar. Third Eye Communications, 2006
*The Lie of Dawns : Poems 1974 – 2008* , Authorspress, 2009
*Land*, Authorspress, 2013
*Hesitant Light* , Authorspress, 2016
*Sky without Sky*, Poetrywalla, 2018

### *Poetry in Odia*
*Bali* (The Victim) Cuttack. Vidyapuri, 1993
*Kahibi Gotie Katha* (I'll Tell A Story), Cuttack. Arya Prakashan, 1995
*Baya Raja* (The Mad Emperor), Cuttack. Vidyapuri, 1997
*Tikie Chhayee* (A Little Shadow), Cuttack. Vidyapuri, 2001

*Chali* (Walking) , Cuttack. Vidyapuri, 2006

*Jadiba Gapatie* (Even If It's a Story) , Cuttack. Friends Publishers, 2008

*Smruti Pari Kichhiti* (A Small Memory) , Cuttack, Bijayini, 2011

### Others

*Orissa,* New Delhi. Lustre Press, 1973

*Poemas* (in Spanish), Campeche. Instituto de Cultura de Campeche, Mexico, 1994

*Orissa* (in Spanish), San Jose. Editorial Montemira, Costa Rica, 2009

*Gale Encyclopedia of Contemporary Authors* (Short Autobiography of Mahapatra), Michigan, 2009

Translations of Mahapatra from Odia and Bengali (to be collected from the poet himself)

### Short Stories

*The Green Gardener*, Hyderabad. Orient Longman, 1997

### Essays & Memoirs

*Door of Paper*, New Delhi. Authorspress, 2006

*Bhor Motira Kanaphula* (in Odia), Bhubaneswar, Paschima, 2011

### SECONDARY SOURCES:

1.   Jayanta Mahapatra interviewed by N. Raghavan, *Tenor,* 1 June, 1978, pp. 59-64.
2.   Ibid.
3.   Ibid.
4.   *Contemporary Authors' Autobiography Series*, Vol-1, No-II, p.138.
5.   Keki N. Daruwalla (Ed.), *Two Decades of Indian Poetry*— 1960-1980, Vikas Publishing House, 1980, p.113.
6.   *International Quarterly*, Vol.l, No-II, p.200.
7.   *Contemporary Authors' Autobiography Series*, Vol. l, No-II, p.139.
8.   Ibid. pp. 141-142.
9.   *Indian Literature,* Vol.36, No.4, July-August 93, p.58.
10.  Keki N. Daruwalla, "Pain that Moves the Bell", *Poetry Review* Vol.83, No. 1, Spring-93, p.66.

11. K.N. Daruwalla (Ed.), *Two Decades of Indian Poetry— 1960-1980*, op.cit., p.118.

12. Krishna Rayan, "A Study of Mahapatra's 'Relationship', *The Literary Criterion*, Vol.26, No. 1, 1991, p.61.

13. *Contemporary Authors' Autobiography Series*, p.140.

14. D. Dhawan (Ed.), *Indian Literature Today*, Vol.II, p.166.

15. Bruce King, "The Shapes of Solitude", *The Poetry of Jayanta Mahapatra: A Critical Study*, Sterling Publishers Pvt. Ltd., New Delhi, 1986, p.14.

16. *World Literature Today*, Vol.61, No.3, Sun, 1987, p.491.

17. *The Toronto South Asian Review*, Vol.5, No.2, 1990, p.87.

18. S. C. Harrex, "Indian Selections: Review of The False Start", *CRNLE Reviews Journal*, No.2, 1993, p.17.

19. Norman Simms, "A Poet of Many Worlds", *The Poetry of Jayanta Mahapatra : A Critical Study*, Ed. Madhusudan Prasad, op.cit., pp. 36-37.

20. Ibid. p.26.

21. John Oliver Perry, "Approaching Mahapatra's Temple", from *Framing Literature: Critical Essays*, Eds. N. Rama, B. Gopal Rao and D. Venkatswarlu, New Delhi, Sterling Publishers, 1984, p.76.

22. *The Indian Express*, 25th June, 1991, p.12.

23. Madhusudan Prasad (Ed.), *The Poetry of Jayanta Mahapatra : A Critical Study*, Sterling Publishers, New Delhi, 1986, p.49.

24. *Litterit*, Vol. 10, No. 1, June, 1984, p.49.

25. K. Ayyappa Panikar, "The Poetry of Jayanta Mahapatra", *Indian Literature in English*, Madras, Anu Chitra Publications, 1989, p.49.

26. Vilas Sarang (Ed.), *Indian English Poetry Since 1950 : An Anthology*, Hyderabad, Orient Longman, 1989, p.31.

27. Sahu Nandini. *Recollection as Redemption*. Authorspress, 2005.

# A Rain of Rites

Sometimes a rain comes
slowly across the sky, that turns.
upon its grey cloud, breaking away into light
before it reaches its objective.

The rain I have known and traded all this life
is thrown like kelp on the beach.
Like some shape of conscience I cannot look at,
a malignant purpose in a nun's eye.

Who was the last man on earth,
to whom the cold cloud brought the blood to his face?
Numbly I climb to the mountain-tops of ours
where my own soul quivers on the edge of answers.

Which still, stale air sits on an angel's wings?
What holds my rain so it's hard to overcome?

# A Sailboat of Occasions

Tall sails hesitate, rise on the masts,
filled with the swagger and prowess
of the evening wind. Rough tactics.
Like the deck your small look tilts and sways.

What you would have wanted to show the world
is your stagnant silence that falls away
from the wind. Bleak that adorning figurehead
which faces the great empty sea around.

And you were all concerned for lack of life,
for having ignored the beneficence of the sky
and the waves, with their solemn assumptions.
Humbled by the ghostly threat of the wind's flight.

On that boat which carries nothing anywhere
the dark winds ought to have known:
of the world which could slip down into that sea
of the taut-wide eyes of a lost child,

of your wife's role made for savage solitude.
Inside maybe, the noises spin, like gull cries,
like the love of other men. And the bare sails
dance, sudden canvas and whole exile of your day.

# A Wind of Judgment

The flock of white swans is asleep in its arms,
the ruined temple across the darkening fields
quite unaware of a thousand eager footsteps;
and beyond the last sky the clouds that wait

appear friendly and disarming as children,
before getting away with the savagery of a sudden storm.
What  legend of life can exist without
the privileges of danger shared, our being inhabited

by desire or envy or regret?
Yet these are there, standing obscenely as stones
against the light, every one of them
a bruise to the wind, an ambushing of the breath.

Once my pain seemed strange, as though
lost by my absence; it was easy to make renunciation,
thinking of taking to wing on an animated wind.
Was I afraid of lonely windows set high

in walls of stone? The exotic ships silently lining
the wharves along the river
caught in ecstasy on the calm wind? A layer
of fierce dust now, blown by the wind, of unbelievable
success,

runs the sharp outlines of face, home and shrine
greyly into the sky. I watch your face take on
its expression of tender concern in quiet pretense
above the wind's  roaring in the courtyard,

not daring to peer into the darkened  mirror
and hear the blacker deodar leaves
threshing about like angry spirits of the night,
and the swans, secretly snaking up their throats.

■

# Another Hour's Bell

Because pain
is the scent of earth,  unquestionably,
these hours  do not complain
of having to meet,  behind  closed doors,
neither  hearing  nor seeing
those who live in us still:
the lost tracks  wanting  to proclaim
their fear and their dream-
yet no dream  enters  where  the mind  should  be.
Down  by the morning
the town  is quiet,
a child's  game not  to be disturbed,
the market  squares filled with  people,
smoke  flowering  on the riverbank,
as I come  to know
the meaning  of the cool air:
how far away have the wounded winds gone?

My friend,  tell me nothing.
Perhaps past joys,  too,  always  meant
to tell me something
but they never thought it important enough.
Your face shows  no surprise  today
at my look,  even more  indiscreet
than you had remembered it.

Because I hear others
moving  to help,
into  the safety of concern
I imagine  they feel-
and on  the wary  winter air
hear lightly  the soft  muted  tone
of another  hour's  bell,
moving  cold and clear.

# Ash

The substance that stirs in my palm
could well be a dead man; no need
to show surprise at the dizzy acts of wind.
My old father sitting uncertainly three feet away

is the slow cloud against the sky:
so my heart's beating makes of me a survivor
over here where the sun quietly sets.
The ways of freeing myself:

the glittering flowers, the immensity of rain for example,
which were limited to promises once
have had the lie to themselves. And the wind,
that had made simple revelation in the leaves,

plays upon the ascetic-faced vision of waters;
and without thinking
something makes me keep close to the walls
as though I was afraid of that justice in the shadows.

Now the world passes into my eye:
the birds flutter toward rest around the tree,
the clock jerks each memory towards the present
to become a past, floating away
like ash, over the bank.

My own stirrings like the wind's
keep hoping for the solace that would be me
in my father's eyes
to pour the good years back on me;

the dead man who licks my palms
is more likely to encourage my dark intolerance
rather than turn me
toward some strangely solemn charade:

the dumb order of the myth
lined up in the life-field,
the unconcerned wind perhaps truer than the rest,
rustling the empty, bodiless grains.

# Dawn

Out of the dark. it whirls back
into a darkly mysterious house.

Is it the earth within?
Does it keep us waking, give brief respite?

Like a hard crossword puzzle
it sets riddles against one another:

the thunders trailing around hatchet-faced banana leaves,
a front gate limp with dew,

the acid sounds of a distant temple bell,
the wet silent night of a crow that hangs in the first sun.

Is the dawn only a way through such strange terrain?
The frenzy of noise, which a silence recalls

through companions lost, things suddenly found?
There is a dawn which travels alone,

without the effort of creation, without puzzle.
It stands simply, framed in the door, white in the air:

an Indian woman, piled up to her silences,
waiting for what the world will only let her do.

# Desire

Down into the meaningless valley the river runs.
Somewhere in the distance my snaking eyes

pause at the coming of dawn, the waters
no more than a shadow of the original flood

that held up the old, mossed stone banks.
Here the sullen water rubs softly on the mind.

And something makes one tired. Even death-ashes,
half-burnt logs and tombs of urns make no sense.

Remember the mean, stiff face of that god
in his shrine? The smell of guilt at the beginning?

What makes one wait? The water dies among the harsh faces
of the flowers that had tipped blood through the night.
They don't trust me any more with their colours, their light.
Why does the dawn appear impatient, groping

as though with stretched arms to clutch the silence of my
being?
Or is it only desire, hoping to resume its inner light,

when our hands, like sad, surprised little lamps
try to hold the spangles of darkness we have learnt to lose?

# Doors

So many  doors  before me,
and each single one open.
Yet one cannot  enter,
walking  silently  by a door.
These dead things
loom  larger  with every hour that goes.
I pass the door  beyond  my freedom
and glimpse  my haggard  face.
I look for those who  could  be mine.
I look for those who  once
protected  me by believing in me
when  I  could not  believe in myself.
Listening  to conscience is not  performance.
Within  this  world,  debts  are owed,
and I  would  pay them  out  of fear.
What lay beyond  these doors?
Fossilized specimens, old bones,
mystic carvings  of a religious  past?
All memories  merely,
that would  bring  a price?
The dim light  pulls my life back.
I stare at my door,  overpowered by time.

# Farewell

So to the day standing  between  us
I will say, I must compromise myself because it is
nothing, I shall not
return to the words I have said.

Love,  the sudden  thought of it.
Truth, how  you gave me a fright!
How quiet it is, this design
we are determined to defeat!

I'd like to believe now
I have nothing  to do with you.
Under the bright light of day,
soft moist earth  between  open lips.

And the past plays about,
laughing  silently,
seized by a dread of night.
Your long-silent  words cut my skin,
the sight of my blood
gives a moment's relief.

# Flight

The sadness of the stones.
Perhaps, waiting to rise off the ground,
you will not speak or raise your eyes,
your danger white by this act of your will.

It is the mist which has not lifted still,
the lapping of waves on the shore
as though it were of a dark spirit, of your crimes of old.
Did you hear reassuring shouts across the fog?

Of a voice you seemed to recognize?
Somewhere at the pale sleepy surface of water,
at the level of lichen and grass,
a white wing quavers and floats away,

like a memory that moves out of the dead
and touches you.
It does not seem cold, to your hands.
Over the wet bank its rainbow hangs

like brilliant flames of the hour,
plunging you deep into your eye
where your forgotten guilt casts its shadow
upon the stone, on its darker way down.

# Glass

Something still remains, to put through
the agony of a dream that indicates
merely the direction of my life.
I have been expecting it, uncertain

of how I'd be able to lift my little finger
in defense of my many faces
at the closer threat of life behind the glass.
I wanted to hear the melody of simpler things,

not of transition or revolt or age
or the flight of blood that marked the place
where you surrendered your will to mine.
It's the obscene pallor of lamplight against the sun

that shows me the beginnings of that path
upon which I had set my feet
and slipped. The image I see is mine.
That which has gone has had its place

and now gives nothing but this real in exchange
the days are spilt, and men make me ashamed.
From time to time it reminds me to defend my way
into my dream, hard and dry and clear as glass.

■

# Heroism

As in a film, this talk of freedom,
freedom from want, social injustice and greed,
poised above the bleeding heartland,
fields stretching orange, white and green.
For afterwards,
there will be no sacred relic of democracy,
neither the confusion of concrete and glass
nor tragic nightmare,
no first or last days of human love,
no vanity of victory entering the face
of some one-eyed paranoid man.
All our thousands of hands
that reached out to the sky
sulk in small strips of black cloth
of futile protest on our chests.
And I, writing my poem again,
what do I remember of faith and past hopes?
Mine was the generation that paid homage
to Gandhi and Tagore, saw in my mother
the stare of Dostoyevsky's Grand Inquisitor.
It was the end of the war,
the beginning of the curse of beggardom.
Prophets preached the mysteries of a new kingdom.
Today, when I participate in group discussions
or scour the newspapers every day with urgency,
the words I read and hear

seem simply to walk the globe together,
holding  hands and telling stories-
But no truth  comes down  to the street.
No  believer  has given up his life for freedom.
There  is merely caution  in those words,
weak sentiment, and history
in which  the country's  leaders like to drown.
Never  before  had I been near enough
the danger a word  carried
to appreciate its monstrosity.
The  sky is not my freedom  of speech.
Only  a police jeep cruises by, as in a film,
with the grinning  officer waving at me.
Everyone in our street  knows him;
there is nothing  he can ever do wrong.

# Now When  We Think  of Compromise

At times the sunlight loses its fleeting habit
and with simple fingers touches my feet, as though
it was preparing the place, the sombre earths of a rite.
It is then that we fall silent, feeling a tremor through
our empty hands, forbidden colours telling us
where we want to go.

Far far out, across ten thousand visions, the sun
is a sullen individual of light consigned
to the wild white dawn.
It becomes a struggle where we wait, to let it come,
between the beginnings of life and a transgression.
Can our dreams tell what ambiguities
our natures beg to hold?

We all want to find the man who can rise out of his rite.
And yet we are the ones who'll never let ourselves out,
who hang here and there like decorations
on the walls of our cries.
Now with my terrtble silence I follow
the fingers of a conjurer.
I feel the sunlight assess and judge the shapes of our hands.

■

# Of Independence Day

We have lost those first days
that had crowned  themselves  with  thorns,
the damp  tender  grass growing to sanctuary
on faiths we could not manage  to understand,
we have lost all those stories
about  the rustle of the blood
that caught  its breath  when  the British
seized our laughter
tossing  timelessly for ages
beneath  the time of the sun.
Our  dead too,  among  the scrub on the river bank.
We have lost the pain of making  love,
the mist and the darkness  and the dance
that fumbled  in its air, and
in the eyes of our  women  the dark  prayers
that fluttered  like temple  banners in the sun.
We are careful to say nothing now
to our children  that  might displease
or provoke them.
A Rubik  cube of menace, we feel,
spins carelessly in their immature hands.
"Have  you noticed  how  the grass is empty?"
I ask my son. His fingertips  seem to hold
little tongues  of fire he's unaware of.
This talk about India's freedom struggle
is nurtured because of our own weakness,
the black and white eyes of children say.
And  the ashes of our dead
take the children by surprise,
spurting up suddenly like water.

Today  we creep in
surreptitiously into  the house and pull
our  memories  of the dead in after us;
the computer's increasing  sound
cannot  be drowned by mere noises of the dead.
Perhaps this was the song of the earth
going  to ruin our  children  are getting  into,
to amuse themselves  and arrive.
But with  the child's  pulse of our past,
how  could we be strong  and aggressive  and free?
The  thought of buried  treasure
still seemed like a confirmation
of a form,  a voice to us-
but where  was it that one could hide?
It's only  the children  perhaps
who can find a place outside  of both good and evil.
Like Roshanara,  eyes hidden  behind  dark glasses,
bearing down  with  the sun's  arrogance.
Or  because India always  wanders.
The  trouble  is:
the dead extend their hands,
but the children  are alarmed
by the nude,  ghastly  bones.
The sun runs on without seeing or hearing,
and we have hung  out
the carcass of the past in the crossroads:
our children  keep seeing
our fingers  pulling  shreds of meat from  it.

# Pain

The dark tree that stands
over the fidds of my blood
has failed to leaf and bud.

Why  must it cut across my blood?
I must try to understand  it well.

Pursued again and over again
by the sky's heights,
it holds itself fast to the mist of time,
giving my mind little rest, small shelter.

Where  are the inessential leaves
that commanded the heart,
disturbing  those clouds which only are
the secrets of the sky?

When  will my eye return,
that has been swallowed by the sky?

What  ceremony
veils its world?

# Shadows

Trying  to fall back on light's considerable status
my mind would escape all the living shadows.
For do they reach me more just to hide my ignominy?
Or to make me some sort of a traitor to my ways?

It is the sun that amazes with its range of airs,
its skies confusing me with the richness of bursts;
often I feel the angry silence stirring the lotuses,
and the waters buried in the earth going white.

Wonderful the light bounding from tree to tree,
quiet and smiling, a gospel's pure murmur.
And yet is the only purpose of light
to fill evening with sighs, set a universe adrift?

Waiting, shadows descend eventlessly from the trees.
They move forward, smelling of sweat and blood,
over disguise and presence, with piercing certainty
to loosen the fragments from the breathings of the light.

What fallacy of light do they leave behind?
Is this what each shadow is for,
to make me dare the open center of the heart's space
drowned in the longings of my weaknesses?

Perhaps one's own world one will only fall back upon,
(the light unlocking its shadows which will not understand it)-
those coming along the quiet emptiness of a life,
empty shell or husk that holds the seed of light: a paradise.

# Song of the Past

My life lies in this shallow slough in the hills,
refusing one the courage of taking to flight,
testing the mind for communion with  the dead;
a past that uncoils itself and alters

into the statue of an aboriginal wooden being
who plays on one's fear of being afraid.
Or, is my indefinable mother  who  merely
sits around  not knowing  what to do,

fetishes hidden away in her common eyes,
but with the faith of a dark-limbed naked child
who draws the whole world close against her.
I have become used to this colorless haze,

and like the sun, sink flatly and slowly into it,
become used to the belief that nothing can be said,
inside the sad and hunched sermon of defeat.
Perhaps it is easier to live on this way,

with the measured stars
that sink the evening's  teeth into my skin,
the past which still sears the shadowy field
of childhood  among  the beasts of darkness and death.

Is it the ghost of a river in my blood?
Or the eerie wind which laps the waters,
secretly searching for the smell of blood
as it drips over the stone so sacred to our fetish?

What is real is this
wistful dreaming about the axis of the past,
and this my body, like a law of gravity,
held forever, lost in insistent earth and fire.

And time, which slowly makes us forget our misery
for the emptiness in our own mouths,
falls upon my bowed head, an overripe melon on a vine:
its back of clay keeps an old habit going.

# The Day After My Friends Became Godly and Great

The clock ticks wildly against the widening dawn.
The pigeons flutter from the window beyond my vision.
The trunk full of old papers and things
distresses me like dead men; quietly something lingers on

the door like history through which they have gone,
I do not wish for the road that stretches sullenly behind.
Terrible, puffed-up clouds swoop upon the sky
and yet leave no trace in the soft blue.

The reflection in the mirror
robs me of the use of my nibbling mind.
Yet what can it do without me?
There are those friends I have not seen for years,

and when the sun sets the worn-out world on fire again,
isn't there this feat, the offering of one's own nerve
that pulls on the rays, to achieve some happiness?
What must come, speaking of impossible things,

is an indulgence,
that covers the festival of life with unadulterated time;
the dead hours of reason that turn against the heart's napalm,

or restlessly spell the minutes outside of you
to die around that whore you even cannot have.

It is memory only that makes one a silent part.
The simpler life makes you forget the cold purpose of your walk.
What use is history if it gives sanction to certain things?
Or if I try to hide my mysterious road from the hour's edge,
the one which held my dispirited friends?

■

# The House

A child's first drawing with a door
through which clouds enter, a promise of life.
Every house is the same; the first days, the believing,
and the thought that somewhere someone
is always waiting for his dream.

From the beginning you are awake in its order of rest
its air entitled to get your serious attention.
Later perhaps you find a house is not a plaything,
the chance of its being so a mere hypothesis.

Who doesn't devote more of his time to his house?
You hold the walls tightly against your shoulder,
think of lifting it up in your arms
at the first death lying there, there as though in wait for you.
And yet, the house stares at you in silence,
like a corpse itself Your dreams do not seem to function,
wandering vaguely in the dark comers of the present,
as in a body that lies shamelessly without a head.

But bring in a lie when you are sure
no one is watching, some dishonesty or a scheme of adultery;
such things will tie the house to black secrets
making you grow in strength

for the loneliness of the house's next day.
Then, isn't it someone with whom you make friends?
In time won't you sense the danger spots on the walls
and know when the door assumes a false look of tranquility?

And surprised at finding it, suddenly, unhealthy
but enjoyable. Usually it ought to have held you
by the dream, by the far-off sunlight that comes
running through the streets, pushes open the door,

to hug the cat sleeping peacefully on the floor.
Is your heart torn by a secret apprehension
finding the kind of company you've got into?
Perhaps here is your real life;

its ghosts outline your covert face against the house,
unwilling to let your time slip away unused
from you, but facing that closed relentless door
and the criminal court in session behind.

# The Moon Moments

The faint starlight rolls restlessly on the mat.
Those women talking outside have clouds passing across
their eyes.
Always there is a moon that is taking me somewhere.
Why does one room invariably lead into other rooms?

We, opening in time our vague doors,
convinced that our minds lead to something never
allowed before,
sit down hurt under the trees, feeding it simply because
it is there, as the wind does, blowing against the tree.

Yet time is not clairvoyant,
and if it has the answer to our lives, proud
in its possession of that potential which can change our
natures,
beating the visions of childhood out of us,

the socialism and the love,
until we remain awkwardly swung to the great north honour.
What humility is that which will not let me reveal the real?
What shameful secret lies hidden in the shadows of my moon?

All these years; our demands no longer hurt our eyes.
How can I stop the life I lead within myself?
The startled, pleading question in my hands lying in my lap
while the gods go by, triumphant, in the sacked city
at midnight?

■

# The Storm

All along you are aware
of its dark cloud as it ghosts the air:
the wet flit of fireflies, the early wind's unease,
a world of small manifestations laid bare.

And when it bursts open at last,
your ears ringing with the bells
of heat and unquiet,
whipping up the waters and fields of some sleep,
your faded hopes and horizons,

as the blade of a plough
gleams in the dark expanse of earth,
even then you wouldn't know what it means:
love or hate,
the question you'd be asking yourself.

The dark maw of its approach
vacillating inside you, striking some atavistic chord.
A time when the earth-blood
quivers in the struggle to live,
a certain hunger, the purpose of giving pleasure.

Later, the moon would rise, blood-red,
lighting the soul's edge like a flame.
Later, as the night grows warmer,
and the dead insects stir
on the floor of your flesh.

No manner of restraint then
would prevent unopening the knotted bit of mind
and let it give accord
to the spent fury of the wind,
the collapse of each caress.

And marked by a freshly-felled tree of hope
you shout into the sudden calmness of the air,
to hear your own presence open like a door
and the whining sickly song
of your blood drift past.

# The Whorehouse
# in a Calcutta Street

Walk  right in. It is yours.
Where  the house smiles wryly  into the lighted street.
Think of the women
you wished to know and haven't.
The faces in the posters, the public hoardings.
And who are all there together,
those who put the house there
for the startled eye to fall upon,
where pasts join, and where they part.

The sacred hollow courtyard
that harbours  the promise of a great conspiracy.
Yet nothing you do
makes a heresy of that house.
Are you ashamed to believe you're  in this?
Then think of the secret moonlight of the women
left behind their false chatter,
perhaps their reminding  themselves
of looked-after children and of home:
the shooting stars in the eager darkness of return.

Dream children, dark, superfluous;
you miss them in the house's dark spaces, how can't you?

Even the women  don't  wear them-
like jewels or precious stones at the throat;
the faint feeling deep at a woman's  centre
that brings back the discarded things:
the little turnings of blood
at the far edge of the rainbow.

You fall back against her in the dumb  light,
trying to learn something  more about women-
while she does that she thinks proper  to please you,
the sweet, the little things, the imagined;
until the statue of the man within
you've  believed in throughout the years
comes back to you, a disobeying toy-
and the walls you wanted to pull down
mirror only of things mortal, and passing by:
like a girl holding on to your wide wilderness,
as though it was real, as though the renewing voice
tore the membrane of your half-woken mind
when, like a door, her words dose behind:
"Hurry,  will you? Let me go,"
and her lonely breath thrashed against your kind.

# The Wound

It is dark and cold,
and the rain-water slashes the streets.
In the neighbouring house a child whimpers
for a while, then all is quiet again.
It is the silence which says the world is not ours.

When in the dawn's terrible hour
we awake, weary
of the last thrust of blood in the night,
touched by the fear that leaped out of the dark,
do we dare ask of one another those questions

that go on searching
the secret places of the soul?
Do we open ourselves, fully, ever,
for the moments of love and death
to echo off the hidden wound in the darkness?

Perhaps it would be best
to discover it, some time,
and show it to all the world.
Perhaps the child knows it, sacred relic,
growing up with the helplessness and the generous tears.

We have been hearing the voices through the night,
the applause of the stars,
the existing structure of order,
the great battle-cry throwing us into breathless despair
for making us fight against it in our lives,

as we fumble with our fingers
for the unfathomable  rivers,
the old terror of water where bleeding skeletons
keep crawling  through  the mists,
and the grey walls of our rooms
persist like obscene wounds in the mind's geometry;
the silence that could be a modest dream
writhing  up from the casual knife,
raw by too much sensousness,
ununderstood  absence.

■

# Bone of Time

Is this why one always remembers:
the autumn  night struggling with its breath,
the fireflies pulsing and drawing back
to reveal the fallen teeth of the jungle;
and the moon, to whom we owe
the tempests  of light among the shadows,
seeking refuge
in a narrow window of our wakefulness.
The last time I saw you, I told myself:
I would see nothing, never again;
and the evening stars  that fall to earth
can make the distance between  us no shorter.
Your window looks so warm from here,
and the wind drifts away noiselessly
across the comfortless  river;
bone of time
that makes each one understand
how night is night; and through it
to enter  the kingdom where Orion  turns,
calm and certain, into neither  darkness  nor light.

# Hands

Between them
a silence occupies the whole place.

Slowly my body has walked
into deep water.

As a boy I learned to come in
by the back door. Sad
houses now, clean and leaning
against one another, full of sleep.

My old rag elephant is
smothered with small screams.

From the dark surface,
waving like grass-
When the last boat crosses the lake.

# I Hear my Fingers Sadly Touching an Ivory Key

Swans sink wordlessly to the carpet
miles of polished floors
reach out
for the glass of voices

there are gulls crying everywhere
and glazed green grass
in the park with the swans
folding their cold throats.

# Sanskrit

Awaken  them;  they are knosps of sound
that seem to melt and crumple up
like some slack jellyfish of tropical seas,
torn  from sleep with  a hand  lined  by prophecies.
Listen  hard;  there  male gaunt  world sprawls  the page
like rows of tree-trunks reeking  in the smoke
of ages, the branches glazed and dead;
as though longing to make up with  the sky,
but  having lost touch  with  themselves
were  unable  to find themselves, hold meaning.
And yet, down  the steps into the water at Benares,
where  the lifeless bodies  lie, resolved  of the problem
of life's coherence, in their  weary wreckage,
the shaggy  heads  of the word-buds move back and forth
between the sentimental swishing of rain
and  the hard,  priest-ridden disfavours of summer-
aware  that their  syllables' overwhelming silence
would  not escape  the hearers  now,  and which
must  remain  that  mysterious divine path
guarded by the queer,  quivering banyan trees:
a language  of clogs over the cobbles, casting
its uncertain spell, trembling sadly into  mist.

■

# Summer

Not  yet.

Under  the mango tree
the cold ash
of a deserted  fire.

Who  needs  the future?

A ten-year  old girl
combs her mother's hair
where crows of rivalries
are quietly  nesting.

The  home will never
be hers.

In a corner  of her mind
a living green  mango
drops  softly to earth.

# Waiting for the Tenth Month and After

As simple as a drop of water
wearing out
the long looks
we fill with each other
before it falls
to the ground

and discover
that the blood-gifted look
rising in a cry
bears little resemblance
to either yours
or mine

One flesh perhaps
made this stir
toward innocence
long unfelt

# Taste for Tomorrow

At Puri, the crows.

The one wide street
lolls out like a giant tongue.

Five faceless lepers move aside
as a priest passes by.

And at the street's end
the crowds thronging the temple door:
a huge holy flower
swaying in the wind of greater reasons.

■

# A Missing Person

In the darkened room
a woman
cannot find her reflection in the mirror

waiting as usual
at the edge of sleep

In her hands she holds
the oil lamp
whose drunken yellow flames
know where her lonely body hides

# Listening to a Prayer

Stone cuts deep

A bell trembles,
touched by the pain
of countless people

Across the temple square,
the wind
that settles on my shoulders
has nowhere to go:
neither a silence
nor an answer

# Three Indian Poems

1
The childhood never leaves us.
A fire warms only those
who have their arms to trust.

2
These brick-batted roads of violence
which go on breathing after dark,
I can feel the air that wounds.

3
Schools too, rest on silence.
What is childhood then?
Like lepers dragging legs
louder than words,
all dead
the simple meat.

■

# Silence

I have read the silence
that dances across the land at dawn.

I have watched it grow
from a small lonely window.

It hurts.
The hundred thousand eyes.

When I try to get over it
it creeps into my bed like a furtive child.

Is it really the waiting I've known?
Words clinging to me like a trick?

Nobody can help me
if I pull the covers over it.

Was it not on the inside,
walking down ahead of me in the morning?

# Myth

Years drift sluggishly through the air,
is a chanting,  the long years, an incense.
Face upon face returns  to the barbed horizons
of the foggy temple; here lies
a crumpled leaf, a filthy scarlet flower
out of placeless pasts, on the motionless stairs.
                    Old brassy bells
moulded by memories, dark, unfulfilled,
to make the year come back again-a recurring prayer.
                    The stairs seem endless lifelong,
     and those peaks too, Annapurna, Dhaulagiri;
uncertain, impressive as gods.
                    I dare not go
into the dark, dank sanctum
     where the myth shifts
swiftly from hand to hand, eye to eye. The dried,
sacrificed flowers smile at me. I have become;
                    a diamond in my eye.
Vague grieving years pit against the distant peaks
like a dying butterfly
                    as a bearded, saffron-robed
man asks me, firmly:
                    Are you a Hindoo?

■

# An Old Country

Dead grandfathers lift their heads and watch.
They will not speak, politely silent, under protest.

All the wounds litter the sky or lie like craters
high up in the mountains, like laughing children.

Looks can embarrass  them, even delirious dreams.
At times they cry out in their silence, calling upon
saints and gods, and they keep asking questions.

Why do they go on asking questions?

Anything is better than the strangled  pain,
the puttering  around  the garden's  obese flowers,
hands in the soft generous grass, curled
like question marks.

# Servility

The grave flood rushes past,
as it had
thousands of years ago.

The rain of our conduct
rings fabulous bells
in the enchanted ears of peacocks
in the jungles of dark shrines.

An owl
stares on at our narrow world.
Something simply dissolves.

The miles of black water
reveal the empty course of performance:
balls of cooked rice to appease the dead.

# Ikons

Black ikons:
a museum of symbols
silence the land.

Swale mists
still blot out the hills.

And illusion:
the sacred plant in a Hindoo home,
cow and scabbed stone,
a dark rock of answers and air.

What else can the face of crowds, show?

Among them a father stands,
looking around, like a hill.
Then, mumbling to himself,
he touches the *lingam* with his forehead,
divine earths closing his eyes, a sighdess god;
his charred silence
left from an enormous fire
no one can remember.

# The Abandoned British Cemetery at Balasore, India

This is history.
I would not disturb it: the ruins of stone and marble,
the crumbling  wall of brick, the coma of alienated decay.
How exactly should the archaic dead make me behave?

A hundred and fifty years ago
I might have lived. Now nothing offends my ways.
A quietness of bramble and grass holds me to a weed.
Will it matter if I know who the victims were, who survived?

And yet, awed by the forgotten dead,
I walk around them: thirty-nine graves, their legends
floating in a twilight of baleful littoral,
the flaking history my intrusion  does not animate.

Awkward in the silence, a scrawny lizard
watches the drama with its shrewd hooded gaze.
And a scorpion,  its sting drooping,
two eerie arms spread upon the marble, over an alien name.

In the circle the epitaphs run: Florence R--, darling wife
of Captain R-- R--, aged nineteen,  of cholera...
Helen, beloved daughter  of Mr and Mrs J. S. White,  of cholera,
aged seventeen,  in the year of our Lord, eighteen hundred...

Of what concern to me is some vanished Empire?
Or the conquest of my ancestors' timeless ennui?
It is the dying young who have the power to show
what the heart will hide, the grass shows no more.

Who watches now in the dark near the dead wall?
The tribe of grass in the cracks of my eyes?
It is the cholera still, death's sickly trickle,
that plagues the sleepy shacks beyond this hump of earth,

moving easily, swiftly, with quiet power
through  both past and present,  the growing young,
into the final bone, wearying all truth with ruin.
This is the iron

rusting in the vanquished country, the blood's unease,
the useless rain upon my familiar window;
the triumphant smile left behind by the dead
on a discarded anchor half-sunk in mud beside the graves:

out there on the earth's unwavering gravity where it
waits like a deity perhaps
for the elaborate ceremonial  of a coming generation
to keep history awake, stifle the survivor's issuing cry.

# The Day

Like some shape beside my body; a presence, flourishing.
While I keep wanting long into the night,
calling for that moment of feeling.

I keep trying to touch its places, things,
hoping they would touch me back,
perhaps open me up to that I've not seen before.

I wonder if what I'm doing is right,
if the day is all,
is that which holds me firmly to my world.

At times a day of my past
stands in front of me, ethereal as a ghost.
And my body wanders to the dark ends of my story.

Such days are always happening.
And if I had learned from one
all that I was likely to learn, where would it have led me?

No day ever knows the lasso of the sun on my door,
how the darkness races round the edges of the light
to strike a path across the skies I've never owned.

# The Rising

There is a past which moves over
the magic slopes and hamlets of the mind,
whose breath measures the purpose of out lives.

Like a flag it flutters across eternity,
yet when I try to hold it high, to make it
an instrument of my glory,
its call drives me
over the boundary I've built in my flesh.

Its hidden nest
stops the flying bird, the impenitent words.
And is made of dead leaves
that echo the wind coming through,
laden and wide with skies,
that will not divide us from our deaths.

■

# The Mountain

Shackled to the earth it stands,  all its dead weight.
In the darkness of evening,
silence and pressure only,
multiplying,  adding, subtracting,
in the abyssal heart.

Each day,
falling to pieces under the straddling sunlight,
it gives clear proof that one
might still reconstruct  one's  life. Rigid,

yet strangely impotent,
perhaps it waits eagerly for the world to speak,
for the mute clock to strike again,
for a new kind of society to form from the ruins of hate.

And all day
we climb those slopes which do not ease at all,
where unfinished time blots out the differences
among us, as it sets itself irremediably on the peak.

Late in the evening of life
an embarrassment prevents the world from speaking.
Can the wide valley here down below
lessen the mountain's weight? Here,

where we are afraid within ourselves,
and the earth  is thin and sad with insufficiency;
as, above, the wind razes the fields of our rights
and the great bulk of conscience stirs,
moving in its process of exorcism.

■

# Dead River

An unknown bird grays a yellowed weed,
a rope of familiar water
makes a desultory circle round me.

Walking past,
along the rude embankment of rough stone,
this silence opens like a face beneath:

like a father left behind with his picture
of his traceless son, perhaps dead,
gray with determination, and infinite skies.

Now a near-naked man ends his bathe
exorcised by the generations
between his folded palms, a ghost of morning.

I hold up my silence, but it is no light,
a slow mist still fights the eye
for life's persistent symmetry,

the silted boat that will not move;
tamed temple god, this river,
sluggish centuries curled away from its bone,

and calling men of another world
to hold its destiny in their rueful minds, birth by birth:
a woman, without the body in her mind,
lying prone, dreaming on after all intention had died.

# It's my Room Once Again

It's my room once again,  the accustomed  chair,
those books around  me, the ball-point  in my hand.
Weeks of rain have weakened  the earth,  the corners
of memory  to shudder with a growth  of moss.
The sky so far away, its clouds floating across
like men with dark faces being led into prison.
The sound  of a wet garment  beaten  against  a stone.
Last night's  news bulletins strewn  upon  the wet streets.
And I've been trying not to mark time in here.
But all of them keep coming into my room,
and  I find myself in a breathless  silent tableau,
a game of  speech  in which I invariably lose.
I can feel the words  coming between  us. Or was it space?
Was it a blindness that pushed  my body
against  each breath  of mine, a laughter  in every  voice?
A knot of unspoken words  slides down  my throat.
I do not know what I want: I ape a poet's  poise,
in my soiled shirt as though  it were empty  of its body,
as though  what  was inside  was all thin mind;
and I ape the stone of my fathers: bland  eyes,
meek shoulders,  to take whatever  might come.
Here, wasn't  this pure deceit? I see them  all
trying hard  not to stare at me, in their midst,
and  I shake my head sadly, get up from the chair
to walk over to the window - before my hour -
my feet firmly braced upon  the floor, and  feeling how
just pretending as if I were on stage could  be enough,
knowing  I could say no more, or be someone special,
or lived like them  rather  than thought. And lost.

# The Looking Glass

In front of me is a world
that doesn't seem to care.
Sunlight that's brilliant as ever.
And someone who hasn't heard my name at all.

Here my hands merely open and close.
My face hasn't moved all night.
My fallow feet, awake side by side,
senselessly rub the air with their toes.

I lift my head and look,
but there's no one there.
I'd like to wait and wait
until my head drops back again.

Still I do not know what I want.
I like to be here a long time
but that wouldn't help me to make sense.
I'm not sure I know myself yet.

And I try to stand and bear my pain.
I can hear the beating of my heart
but my body doesn't seem to move.
Only the quick steps of my blood go past me.

And I follow myself around,
piece by piece, everywhere.
The world is always at the end, there.
With sunlight shaking the carcass of last night.

# At Shivaji's Fort at Panhala:
# Looking  Across the Western Ghats

Late afternoon, embroidered rockface,  the sun's  glow
spreading  strange  light everywhere;
over  the upraised  blade in the crossroads  of the Fort
bleeding its dreams  still, tracks  of death
between legendary  Baji Prabhu's eyes,
over  the luminous  Kumbi and  Kasari  that  wander,
their old banks  scored by  the untamed  hooves  of the Marathas-
and  the huge plain below  beginning  to swell and  rise.
Through  the thickness of the sod  part of the voice I've climbed
            up to hear
gets lost,  a slow  tolling sometimes  heard,  then  unheard;
the horizon  reels away  as though  sick and  dying
from  the last rasp of battered  stone  walls, finally subdued.
What  tale did I wish to carry  back  to my homeland?
Walking  painfully  up,  realising how one gets tired
of the word: history,  the enthroned stone,  its vain  brown  eye
mottled  with intimacies  of a shifting  civilisation.

Today I sit and  watch  a world  safely from  the cliff-edge;
revealed  on the hostile surfaces  of time
I think  of how  a thing might move in the cause of justice
immobilising  the hour  to bring  together  in memorable
silence the endless postures  of a royal  warrior;
as I wander,  by chance,  in that  hour

among the unrecognisable fragments of princely citadels
and houses of gambling and whoredom, abandoned to
that solitude not knowing where one had gone nor
where was one to go.
And yet how the barren January wind catches one in
ecstasy on the grim Pusati hillside!
As the deep red ovals of light dance from treetop to treetop
in the clear calls of bulbuls across the scarred valley!

For here was the hour from which one might grow:
the rich black mould that gave promise of wild fertility,
when the great plain beside the Sahyadri flamed to flower
with the blood of the day of the dead and rested satisfied.
The century's storm has died down. My hands kiss rock,
seek the meek combs of rust on the stone. And
            the blood-red sun
Js simply the mask of a child who dances away for us, evening
            after evening.

And the leaking dust from the cracked granite of the fort
just an invisible presence, air that knocks every little vertebrae
under the skin. Human as I am, I seek asylum elsewhere,
dreading the sadness disembowelled time has cast upon the
            stone's mind.
A slender stalk of grass in a crack seems like a monster to
            wrestle with.
Beyond, the endless plain rises slowly to the dark
with the darkness that draws blood from the green breath
of narrow-waisted grasses, for that haunted light
when the lame and fallow fields of history learnt to wield
that enchanted sword, their plain's great peace.

# Bhopal Dawn

Dawn-like, the page lies open, white.
What is it that remains of one's life?
Words? How strange it seems today
to have loved a rag doll sometime.

Trapped inside, dreams
build still, tense into the light.
Earth passes by. Always to the right
a star appears, freezes sight: memory.

This page, what can it be
but un-understanding, a mere object
or perhaps nothing? If I could have,
I'd have gone back. Not watched helpless
a track of light widen on the air.

Night is where slavish stars move,
where darkened roads grip the heart
in dumb cries of rage and fear.
Yet one falls back on the idea of happiness,
balancing oneself, with words, a spinning top.

The earth beneath is cold. A lost ray
starts slipping toward the east,
weaving sunrise. A word becomes a plot.
The page of life sprouts scary, unseeing eyes.

# Predicament

Dear Runu, everything moves here
but nothing really comes.
The children play their games,
but they belong somewhere else.
In the mirror the image stays:
the sky, the street, the park.
The branches ache, heavy with fruit,
the birds vanish, ageing with silence.
But as always, nothing comes.
The geckos chuckle on the walls,
mushrooms sprout on damp earth,
and when I awake,
it is neither day nor night.
Perhaps when something comes
I am asleep, and like a lie of living,
it keeps dancing on my bed.
It has been so since long;
all of them feel bound to say something,
anything comforting.
But they do not come, pushing
each other out of their fear.
Even an old song is lost
as it approaches this silence.
There is just the lonely mirror,
feeding on life, on shadows of the past.
And absence is like a child's puzzle
abandoned to an indifferent adult world.

# A Grey Haze Over the Ricefield

A grey  haze  over  the ricefield.
The black cow grazing with  her  newborn calf,
long-legged, unsteady –
or trucks  going  past  the high  road:
such  things  only  claim
that  I am looking  out  in search  of memory,
not death. Those  little kisses  on my cheeks
my long-dead grandmother gave  me, or
the soft dampness of my tears  when
my mother didn't  notice  me
from  beyond the closed  door  of her  youth.

Today  the dangling thread stops  halfway down,
where my hands cannot  touch  it.
It's not that  I wait  for judgement.
But at times  I see a shadow
move  slowly  over  these, a shadow freed
from  the past  and  from  the future,
that  contains the footsteps of that  childhood
so light  I can only  think  of squirrels
slipping in and  out  of the mango trees.

■

# Suppose

Suppose it is the third law of Newton.
If I am lost, do I move forward or backward?
Today I have no enemies I know of.
I have no bait to dangle in front of my God.
Merely the will to write a poem to revile God
who has the smile of someone feeding his chickens.
Any explanation for things seems irrelevant.
And my words find it hard to drag their unwilling feet.
Caste riots, or religious riots, are nothing new here.
Or the brutal, senseless killings in the name of God.
Today the mysterious calm is a pattern
that doesn't evoke any questions:
around the seated statue of the Buddha,
under the last suffering,
a new feathered dead
dance by themselves in the shadowless twilight.
Around me the sad silence of a field of chickpeas.
Today I don't know how to hide behind a crowd,
or to make a minute last just a minute, not more.
Truth crumples my life tightly into a ball,
its movement cold and slippery.
The God I had kept hostage to my will as a child
has been stripped of its own skin and face:
I think of parrots screeching in and out of the sky,
my hand on my father's arm
stopping him from going away, and
of the awkward second of my life
that is devised and bound by all of them.

# On the Bank of the Ganges

Along the mildewed magic bank,
stone-eyed trees furred by vermilion
stare savagely like beasts.

The song of a lone Ganga boatman
stumbles across lofty silences.
Pious bathers crowd the riverside steps.

It could be
that the old blind flow
creates a field of force across the mind;
their faces blank and waxen, alive in a dumb impulse,
drawing of touch to be appeased by mystery.

I half-wake from a doze. It is only the wind,
blowing over the water, harsh fire,
that plucks the withered sanskrit flowers on my breath;
while the river lies
with the sullen dignity of an abandoned doll,
used, abused by delinquent children.

And I know I am alone.
Tonight I can remember the lost mornings.
A hawk cries in the gloom:
a purpose on the air, not yet fulfilled.
To be whole, to know how the water lies.

■

# Shadow

Maybe this shadow of mine was born before I was
Now I am never alone because it's always there.
People come often, stopping by for my shadow.
It's not me that draws them here.
They say it's less sensitive
than me and doesn't mind
being tickled or taunted.
It understands what people want.
I feel lost in is silence,
the odd one out.
It isn't ever frightened, or hurt;
there is no defeat in its eyes.
Sometimes it looks so dignified;
a keeper of terrible mysteries.
The bitter presence is my body,
which takes the path straight
to the silent immensity of light.
I can't leave my shadow behind,
It's the only sign I recognize.
I know I can't get ahead of it.
Eventually when I come
not to be aware of it,
the freedom I hoped for isn't there.
And some strange logic
that crawled out at my birth
is down on its knees
before the spectre in its dark cloak.

# The Door

This thing
wakes me like a hand.

Grass waits

and rock
takes the wind's place.

Huge door
drifting
with feet of light,

my eyes
quietly open
before the night's.

■

# A Country Festival

Here yet a country,
the scorching, the slow sleep,
the squalor squealing in despair,
and the inaction dancing in a circle
like naked children round their sheer fingers,
while the darkness dims the air,
old allegories lie oddly, in the hunched postures
of abandoned bones along the river banks.

Long evenings over the burning grounds.
Those places erected through
the years, a place of sacrifice,
so that the pure and virgin might bum
like oil lamps at the feet of cold grey trees.

The evening fosters light,
and kneeling villages inhabit the beginnings
of a tale that never appears to end;
the vague weightiness of chanting
hangs low, sad and restless and black.

And suddenly, then,
like voices, commands, out of the trembling
of the moon, sensing
the presence of tribal ancestors,
a priest's butting nose

explores the silent waste of fears,
conches are possessed by wandering spirits;
and the women,
not answering to their names any more,
and usually lying like unexpected lakes
deep within the wooded hills,
break their calm surfaces
like wild water-snakes let loose
from the yearly Hoods.

■

# Full-Moon Night

Often  a summer full-moon  night has no story
to tell: Of no match  to strike in a gas-filled room

or no lined-up villagers to be shot by militants
resembling a ridge of palms against an unreal sky.

Not even of the emptiness of a butterfly  in metamorphosis
or of a stench  on which to found  some meaningless poem.

But the hero of this story has done  no great crime;
perhaps  small indiscretions or at times a lacquered lie

that presses  down the sad prophetic answers
to questions  as when a rapist crushes  a cowering  child.

So this story shall try to pick up a few brave words,
when even without  a voice we could lose them  all:

a story delivered  from an empty  stage to no audience
because  history is anchored by a dream  of iron that rusts away.

The real hero could be just another woman who sits
with her knees drawn to her chest,  her baby propped

against her shins, hunger withering her impotent flesh,
with the old old behemoth of faith set in Sita's lineage.

But there is no other story here; only the flagrant pain
of wanting nothing more, no rights or longings or loves,

as she unfurls her guts, washes her thirsty shadows,
and drops the unfinished dream of wearying grandmothers

onto the hour; while the full moon falls asleep
over the weary river before they can mate and break free

from the secret morning held unhealed in their throats.

■

# A Morning Walk in Bhopal

A road, going somewhere,
cranking  silence from the morning light
or perhaps from the autumn of my fear.
At times I see someone walking down it
looking at me through the skies of my pain.
That road leads to the edge of earth
where water slips with sad voice and falls.
As though a procession approaches,
moving slowly, to the beat of drums,
returning me to memory as to a hollow silence.

The tatters  of leaves on the roadside trees
remind me of my last innocence.
Now with what longings
shall I  protect my memory?
Whose presence
keeps moving with my breath?
The barren fields' on either side?
The light's sly embrace?

# A Still Winter Morning

A still winter morning, and a sullen mist
playing with the pallor between its fingers.
The only door to an exhausted village hut
opens noiselessly like a tongue hung out.

Just the shadow of a woman
comes and goes
through it into the little vacant yard.
In the corner the scanty harvested paddy
is wet with dew.

Guavas glow green everywhere
with adolescence.
From far down her body,
grief, death, and widowhood,
peer at her old father,
standing like a lost sheep huddled
away from death.

The odor of rats sticks to the sagging floor.
Hunger looks from the middle of a breath.
Once again, it has nowhere to go.
On this still winter morning.
What light there was has not entered her eyes.
Just a woman's shadow up against a wall
of that home of hers so inviolate
it has never opened inside her.

# An Evening by the  River

Dark hills, softening in provocative shadow,
sift like fantasies in this river.
So like the shapes love takes. Here, on the rim
of  the stone embankment,  how often have I
sat and watched  the light  part. From  afar
an unknown  bird's  tense  cry, netting  one
like a scent, suddenly.  And I remember
the value I've placed on you. The slight quiver
of your lips that's almost painful here,
in the momentary  ripple  on the water,
trying to catch the last sparkle of day
before the nightwind sucks and corrodes
the warm hours drifting in the wake of boats
long gone west.

But what makes sense unless one lives in things
made by ourselves? In tales lost, in an absence,
in an awakening  burnt  to ashes
to face this image of my inner sense of defeat?
I recollect the sunlight  rustling  the  leaves
of your eyes, and I stop and retreat underneath
with the moment so I don't  lose it.
When you come back tomorrow, I know, your smile
like the blossoms of this wild creeper on the bank
will merely look about  us, will reveal nothing.
And now beware, the words of this poem say,
of going with it into dream

or of making it seem like the last words of a prayer-
beware of the unreasonable wind inside
that tries to surpass this one which rises now
spiteful and mean, tying the birds
to the trees in the dark.

■

# Dawn at Puri

Endless crow noises.
A skull on the holy sands
tilts its empty country toward hunger.

White-clad widowed women
past the centers of their lives
are waiting to enter the Great Temple.

Their austere eyes stare
like those caught in a net,
hanging by the dawn's shining strands of faith.

The frail early light
catches ruined, leprous shells leaning against one another,
a mass of crouched faces without names,

and suddenly breaks out of my hide
into the smoky blaze of a sullen solitary pyre
that fills my aging mother:
                             her last wish
to be cremated here twisting uncertainly like light
on the shifting sands.

# Days Spent Walking Once

Voices, throwing the moments out of their lives,
saying things before I heard them,
profoundly human. As I arrive
at the railway yard with my seven-year-old son
we see the sliced head like a hairy
watermelon trembling between the rails.
No one in the crowd
had brought in the name of a god
who must be answerable to them yet.

Just one spring morning when the light
was urging us to leap into the horizon,
both of us saw the headless body
growing into uncertainty some distance away,
like the old bridge
down the middle of the river,
one maybe he had left years ago,
the tower he had built once as high as he could,
with his reason winding round and round
to the top in an endless stairway.
We didn't talk; every common word
carried too much terrible weight to be spoken,
so the light gathered on the shore
of the silent city that naked grief owned.
Voices kept on revealing his life story
as a dog leaned forward to lick its sores.

We stood and watched, our Uves suddenly
carrying another life, our living a turbid pool
we could dip from but could not,
with no light to search world s ends for.
I couldn't stand there anymore
as a breath of cold shook the light in his face,
as the spilt blood pointed to a fictitious heroism
making one more alone than one has ever been.
Just one death there, the same world
tumbling over our feet, the growing conviction
that all deaths are Sundays,
their endless fierce fight
pulling the new life out of darkness,
dead words breathing,
but always lonelier than the dead.

■

# Dialogue

The hands that hold this world
have fingers that deep, dying
for uncertain mysteries. Leprous mutilations.
I wish I could break the quiet
of my brother standing near me.
One is not in fear of Dostoevsky's just darkness
that grows between his words.
Or, for that matter, Pasternak's.
I would relax safely in a soft armchair
and watch the show right through to the end,
crossing bridges of hunger and desire,
through the iron hearts of storm and shadow
closing all eyes. The road is waiting,
with the tact and order I need
to protect me from being a murderer.
Deaths lie in my bed in the darkened room.
They come with bloodied thumb-marks
on their throats from children's homes,
from women who take root
like trees in silent fear,
even from the kindest of hearts.
The hands that hold this world
burst out of their slow evil years.

# Elsewhere

In this room of mine
the joy of finding oneself chosen
by the object of my desire
slips from one fear into another;
the laws that govern us
do not see the fantasy of the endings.
Yes, the man walking down the street
knows all about suffering,
crying quietly in his cancer.
His friends smile in awkward silence.
If my suffering is elsewhere,
the morning laughs softly
as it enters the pieces of past time,
and I write a song and laugh too,
thinking desperately to save
the face of the thought I loved.
In this very room I know
my mother pulled her cold shadow
from her breast, wanting to hide journeys
from which she had never recovered.
And my father kept to his strangeness,
in ignorant desire, smelling
the wrinkled sheets in the dark,
not knowing what meaning lay in them.
My room could be a whole world,
and I don't wish to struggle to keep it.
I tum  the page; the simple shepherds

still walk the slopes, and I feel
doors open within me, one by one.

Those altar grounds beyond lie barren,
lthough the blood of human sacrifice
is spilled still, a fantasy
I don't have the strength  for.
I can only leave my shadow to walk
the battlements  of this ruined kingdom;
a sob is merely caught in my throat.
My body speaks with meaning
from the things that could never happen;
it is my own life, Agrippa.
In this room I look at it
with the eyes of a polite childhood
before time looks out of me
and brings back an old tear
in which water found itself too old
to belong to the austerity of ice.
Maybe I look like I have awakened
in a strange bed. In this room
I could dupe myself with the thought
that the world would always be here;
but here I go on making my simple mistake,
as the yearly rains advance and stop,
unable to cross my long closed room.
In darkness my feet find
the familiar worn stairs, stiffening
at the stopped clock of pain
I had told stories of, to myself and others,
during my long life elsewhere.

# Geometry

The old toothless woman in the rain
sitting on the steps of the General  Post Office
stretches out her hand as I pass by
and with the unerring intuition  of her sightless eyes
examines the dropped coin in her palm.
Like a low trick from a conjurer,
her words invoking God's blessings
fall on my ears. Those words had eyes,
and they appeared to stare at me
from a story in a book in a long-buried library.

The wet breeze  hissed at her tangled  hair.
I felt relieved  there  was no one else there;
I'd have been  embarrassed
at having my pity naked before  another.
I remember the weapons  I should  not use,
like self-indulgence, or the curved  mirror  of age
in which the quality of endurance recedes,
getting ever smaller and smaller.

There  I was,
shaking with silence, on an abandoned island
that has revealed  something  of which it is ashamed.
Was it the duty of life to find more than life?
The rain had stopped  its playing,

and I realized  how malignant  was this space
between us, a space of pathetic secrets
that could resurrect a grief again and again,
the terrible geometry  of blood and fire;
of hunger  and the red rag of Puri,
this part of us that groped  with the moaning of roots.

■

# Grandfather

(Starving, on the point of death, Chintamani Mahapatra
embraced Christianity during the terrible famine that struck
Orissa in 1866. )

The yellowed diary's notes whisper in vernacular.
They sound the forgotten posture,
the cramped cry that forces me to hear that voice.
Now I stumble in your black-paged wake.

No uneasy stir of cloud
darkened the white skies of your day; the silence
of  dust grazed in the long afternoon sun, ruling
the cracked and fallow earth, ate into the laughter
          of your flesh.

For you it was the hardest question of all.
Dead empty trees stood by the dragging river,
past your weakened body, flailing against your sleep.
You thought of the way the jackals moved, to move.

Did you hear the young tamarind leaves rustle
in the cold mean nights of your belly? Did you see
your own death? Watch it tear at your cries,
break them into fits of hard unnatural laughter?

How old were you? Hunted, you turned coward and ran,
the real animal in you plunging through your bone.
You left your family behind, the buried things,
the precious clod that praises the quality of a god.

The imperishable that swung your broken body,
turned it inside out? What did faith matter?
What Hindu world so ancient and true for you to hold?
Nervously you dreamed toward the center of your web.

The separate life let you survive, while perhaps
the one you left wept in the blur of your heart.
Now in a night of sleep and taunting rain
my son and I speak of that famine nameless as stone.

A conscience of years is between us. He is young.
The whirls of glory are breaking down for him before me.
Does he think of the past as a loss we have lived, our own?
Out of silence we look back now at what we do not know.

There is a dawn waiting beside us, whose signs
are a hundred-odd years away from you, Grandfather.
You are an invisible piece on a board
whose move has made our children grow, to know us,

carrying us deep where our voices lapse into silence.
We wish we knew you more.
We wish we knew what it was to be, against dying,
to know the dignity

that had to be earned dangerously,
your last chance that was blindly terrifying, so unfair.
We wish we had not to wake up with our smiles
in the middle of some social order.

■

# In the First Rain and Death

A whole wave of stars strangling one another
upsets the dance of a lacework of fireflies in the first rain-
the June evening a drunken bully of the neighborhood -
as time rises up from the hospital dark, the walls,
and from a soaked empty bed about to leap at the throat.

How do you set your little heart going?
With charity evenings, parties for the wounded,
or with the sweet weight of memory escaping from the body
like a maharajah going off to war for a good time?
How the mind is made up to make up a spectacle
of oneself with the world living its game,
signaling its magic from outside through the inevitable glass.

With the stars tied up in knots, soon the evening
is dragged to a doorway to lie at the mercy of its mistrust.
It s this sudden death that pulls one toward it,
lifting up the eyelids, to look at the floating shapes
of paper fireflies drowning in the rain,
only to see our own eyes tethered to the light
and the silent cry of the wave inside starving for air.

# Here and Elsewhere

Rain hours.
Here a young mother has strangled
her only child in the long night.
Fish grow torpid in the ponds.
Elsewhere a woman's squeamishness
seems genuine when she discovers
a caterpillar deep  inside a cabbage.
Elsewhere too a girl is set on fire
for the dowry she did not bring.

Every night I prepare for my walk
in the dusty crowded streets,
where the  marbled  moon breaks  through
the clouds in an ultimate  act of defiance.
Every night frogs appear from nowhere
to mate and croak in the  rain pools.
A scream  drives past through  rainy fog,
a moment  without  past or future.

My father  told me once
about  the old tribes who may have
cut off bits of flesh from young girls alive
and strewn  them  across the  raw furrows
of dark humus  in the Orissa mountains.

Their own reasons for this appeased them;
the men of the tribe  had one another
to fall back upon.  As shadows hovered
over the fields, scrabbling  softly at the light.

Whatever  word I choose  to give it all
spews out a futile lament. Such death
I see everywhere  has to be sold discreetly
in small doses,
and must come to build faith in its own way.
Today my tame  grief is a worn-out
long rope tied at one end,
and God, a conspiracy  for pregnant paddies,
keeps dancing  at the other.

# In this Room

Promises are broken,
voices enter without feelings,
from an unpreparedness that breaks out
from those loved ones when they died,
from the empty time that can listen
to the city's hundred  thousand people
on their way from somewhere to somewhere
and tell itself it's just a dead sky of white.

I remember  my father's hands, playing
then with my mother's false pretense,
the eyes of their room wide open in rage,
while silence would humble itself
and sit down on the wide cold floor,
awed by the smallness of life's secrets
that hold answers to questions we never ask.
And another silence, close by,
strewn around a makeshift church among the trees,
a silence where there is no room to breathe,
as a woman keeps burning, her lost body
breathing fast for a shadow of the sun.

In the middle of our story
I let the wounding air lie close
against my chest. My heartbeat  cannot ease it,
it holds nothing in its hands. The cold light
makes the air harder to breathe.  Outside,
the sky floats past my room
here the world can't get at it;
a bird starts to move, looking
for a quiet place to spend the night.

■

# Late Autumn Afternoon

Snow melts under the rain elsewhere;
Elsewhere, too, the wells dry up in the desert countryside.
Time has no life,
in there only in the courage for a farewell
one needs most,
or in the hope of the hostage looking up
at the sword that will, or will not,
behead him;
time s there in the first careful step
the Taliban jihadi took as he fired
at the fourteen-year Maiala.

It's right to say
time does not exist. It s there simply
to rescue this body that could
possibly rescue time. In the infinities
of disconsolate dreams, in the unexpected tenderness
seen at times in the holocausts
of nature itself, time s own secret sense
begins to pale and fall like the petals
of a full-blown jasmine.

And this grief that deepens at times
and then lessens,
will it show merely a lost path of time?

■

# Like the Blue Haze of Faraway Tea Gardens

Like the blue haze of faraway tea gardens,
the breath  of newborn  jasmines hurts,
scenting  the lost songs of farewell,
While the breeze  goes on struggling  still
in the altar of the old peepal  by the  river.

All around  there  is a rising,
and the hurt of history is not enough,
as it keeps returning in a hundred shapes
like the fugitive cry of a child
I once heard  in a remote  mountain  village
strung  on three  hundred days
of starvation  in a year.

At times I'm like a desperate mother
who has to sell her child
because I can't see her die of hunger.
Nature's  invisible mysteries  moan in shallow mirrors
we do not dare look into.
Here, as a hand,  out of nowhere,
touches  the shoulder  and leaves,
and an endlessness flutters  and bellies
from the curtains  in the windows
terrifying  me:
the chaste words of coming and going,
the hidden  somethings
of our  most secret  selves
that rise in the  mornings  of a voice
and in the arms of mysterious wings.

■

# Loss

It's not the night that sits down beside me
on the steps and tells me what I've lost.
The noon that hung calm midway yesterday
easily imitates the loss of the day before,
when the gentle wind stirred  the grasses
bordering the ricefields and the deep rock,
and the shadows lost their power to shape themselves.

Each loss lingers over my reflection in the present,
like a man who has gone naked so long
that his clothing begins to chafe and bind him.
For when another noon comes,
I know I will be alone
and work my way into the white pages of my enduring
that keep on calling my name without hope.

Past the cemetery the light's beak opens.
A child starts crying in the house next door.
Still I'd like to accomplish and make plans
in this long stretch  of wakefulness.
Today can see only the edges of things, not
substance  or life. When loss
with its deep shadows of painless memories
stamps its footprints into the close air of the future.
Only now and then I seem to feel the wind gathering
in the dark, and the night disappear  into its own shadows.

■

# Making No Secret of Death

The day doesn't realize
how hard this death of mine is,
among the many dressed in white sheets
all ready to hide their disobedience.
We all want love, my friend,
to steady our walk with its pathetic efforts.

This death can't find where my body is;
it is the one death I must keep to myself.
It is I who set this clock running,
and now can't control its movement.
This death is a darkness in which
children keep playing and shouting,
when the sun and trees glow with a chilly light,
and when my childhood no longer exists
and an old forgotten love song
plays out my deepest fears.

A fine rain falls everywhere without
wetting the earth; friends who greet me
move their lips without any sound from them,
and in the dark my soul
is a tired look upon a vast and silent water.

Like a shadow on my footprint, this death shows
where I am. Strange children run in and out
of my room. Someone I know well
will not let me forget myself.

The day sits in the darkness of an unknown city;
its tragedy of light has become so old that
only a sense of faithlessness overcomes one.
Still the day is there,
tossing its silk like a spider,
weaving that net where this death appears,
overcome by the freedom that lies ahead in
the dark, still and shadowy, specter at a feast.

# Needs

The world that gradually spreads like fire
under my needs
has struck the sky's stars.
I am marked by the slow venom of need.

Is an ancient law only to be obeyed?
In the cramped mind where memory
puts its mysterious hand
and gropes between the past and the present?

Again and again some thought
keeps the dawn high above the bared mind,
the details of home, loves and pride
veiled in clouds upon the scales of need,

until, older, one comes to know
that it is not enough to be simply alive,
that the hand reaching out painfully at another
can be caught unawares, drenched  in use's blood.

No man points to the sky
without being aware of the desire to live
in his belly where the earth-snake sleeps.
Dark and plain time-god of freedom and death,

what can make you so sacred?
Which are those needs I can finally reject?
What does the starlight in the gaping distance
know of its resoundings on the sleepless leaves?

There are roaches breeding in the cracks
of my desolate hands of infancy.
And in their merciless eyes
slowly settle the stars of my arrivals and departures.

■

# Old Things to Talk Over

The last light of the sun
kneels with pride once again
on the rice paddies  and village houses
that lie beyond exhaustion.
Martyrdom  is the faceless enemy
who marches  on, thief in the night.
Blind words needlessly  spoken  aloud
in the marketplace come and go,
tasting blood at times,
into silent funeral.

In a hut, hardened by unforgiveness,
an old married couple
races to the surface of time;
they are forgotten,  like many others,
like the last emperor of the  Moguls,
or a pair of worn slippers  hoping someday
to suffer the chaos of fulfillment.

A rainbow lying in the dew
at her feet, the dutiful  daughter
gets ready to fall in love again.
Unending  silence fills the horizon.
Once,  maybe Grandmother, blind,
or blinded then by ritual or cruelty,
could feel her way
in touch with her own lostness;
today the blood falters
in the narrowing veins,
and the fatal threshold has been  stepped over.

Darkness spreads.
Outside, deserted cow-paths wait
for something that does not come;
the earth is doomed once again
to the breathing of torn fields.
Just the stale smell of last week s rice
grows within the walls.

# Rain Poems

## I

In the rain that sails vast spaces
toward the season's end, as a day dies
from the depths of mouthless time,
all movement broken, reeling, drunk, on the winds;
my face is a full white moon
pressed onto the paper-dry surface of dead water.
Thus I approach the boundary between
the voices I make and their drooping echoes,
facing those secrets lost in one's own creation,
now to fold slowly, or rise and fall in turn,
in that inner kingdom of consciousness
which moves each torture of memory into the flesh.


## II

Behind me lie inexhaustible worlds.
Through the window I see the submerged sun
slumped in a medley of grave new ash and bone,
mysterious looking boats on the river's edge,
the noises of charred minds of the past,
the stirred stale air. They are menfolk returning
from a cremation drowsy and rebellious to memory,
their tired mouths lying about the need to themselves,
as they let the rain take over once more,
the waters of thoughts moving along beds
of gravel and grass into an uneven sleep of blood.

## III

Drifting across old scars like a walk
in familiar country, simply celebrates
the abyss of voiceless rain, justifies nothing.
To have the amazement that is a symbol
of what one left, and to return to a condition
for reality: do I know what really is my loss,
doI  know whatI  mean when I say this
while the remembered rain beats against my walls?
This is where the flushed face of unrest
lies waiting for its resolution: to be someone again,
as a window awakens in its strange surge of light,
making magic, like eyes. This lie has no poem.


## IV

All night I have waited for the rain to end,
the forbidden  memories ringing, compelling
footfalls among the ruins, the day's last sun
smoking in unending fields soaked in innocence.
It is the beginning of a voyage that is over,
a weary voice that will not speak or be heard.
Where is that absence which pushed an icy rope
down  my throat,  so close me my heart  could  have  touched  it?
It is a world gone, out of hand, oneI  cannot recognize,
that draws everything  to a close.
Its water rubs softly on my mind;
this water, all the stars' silence, talking to a child.

# Shapes by the Daya

And in these skies, always,
dancing like ghostly light,
the faint cries of cranes and the clouds
floating back to reverie. My hands
that overwhelm me, turn into scarred land
as I stare at them, what is it
that had first touched me? Your silence?
At your touch the sky tilts slowly, and
knowledge is a hollow meaningless sound
that falls from the mouth. A thousand
birds fly to grief in these frightened  winds,
the dark sky shows through  in places.
We have our own passwords, but
who  hears the explosions, the fear
of footsteps leading aimlessly on, to nowhere?
Sometimes our generosity embarrasses us
as though it cannot be stopped, and our
transparent pity-
it's just that we aren't  able
to fold up our skies into a neat stack of papers
where our words dance like the ghastly remains
of long-dead men by the light of a cold moon.

■

# The Absence of Knowledge

A wisp of cloud as though laying siege
to the swollen body of the sky,
or like a puppet breeze moving,
silently stalking the grass at the field's edge.
Here the rains linger on stolid hill slopes,
empires still drag their bloody histories along;
and as I peer into my half-empty shelves,
something there in the dust
that rests on the phantom papers of the past
appears to hold on to the meaning of the world.
I let myself remember
how at a railway station long ago,
I stood at a ticket-window feeling this absence
with unfulfilled hands for a kind of future.
But was it now to be felt
simply as a shape in the dark,
whose features had passed the flush of spring,
an uneasy dove with white, lyrical wings?
Was it some disguise,
a mask I should have killed then,
as it began to destroy what had been built anew?
Today I hear its stubborn voice,
dipping endlessly in and out of sleep.
It is the clock in a grey dawn,
the pain of autumn seeping between bare branches,

the shadow under orphaned children's eyes,
the morning star groaning under
the weight of another night,
it is the dead fish turning up its white belly
in the water once again.
I humble myself and feel it still:
the blank face of a negotiating table

a thousand years old,
the tale handed down
from one generation
to another until it is thrown to the streets.
This ground is jagged with the defeat
of races, of morphines of memories;
huge shadows and dark waters of a lifetime
now come after us, climbing our way.
Once as a child, I realized
I would be watched, identified with performance,
as I went on to learn the face of a man
who leaves one in some dispassionate voice.
The trees around me never moved.
Picking up the morning newspaper,
I encounter a shadow: mine, the fear
of knowing what might be out there,
and its poem, evidence of a pardonable pride.
From the starved earth a silence
rises so incredible it hurts the ears.
The cloud I saw once, bent on suicide.
And the underground  test, pilgrim of a new world,
carrying easily over the distance between us.
It is the same rain now, the same grass;
perched in its dark circle, the dreamless bird
breaking the spirit of trees in waking and sleep.

I always seem to fear it,
because whatever grows from this absence
is the destiny I feel I shall share.
Almost like the past, like God,
moving along the wall like a gecko,
it starts hunting out the bright-eyed insects
freed by rain from the hidden earth of my future.

# The Evening that is to Come

One day
if you suddenly find that the window
you are standing at is untrue,
the colors out of the sky sullen and unwholesome
then it is only the tired wind in your breath
that keeps floating back,
scuffling the hours like dead leaves around you,
of those others
you would have loved to caress in your desire
and whom you are. certain
you can never have
in the hours of your waiting.

This moon
that makes your eyes ache
and is slipping slowly into the trees,
is it heavy
with the shadows of the sun that mock you,
a ghost looking out
for something inside your own aimless breath?
What charity can prevail upon the sky
to drop its sacred blue?

Perhaps
you have had too long a journey to undertake,
the bravery and daring like mindless glow-worms
that  give a false assurance of light along the road;
and perhaps you cannot prevent your moving:
to go down there, where the sounds waken you
to unsettle your birth,
where the tremblings of the earth
that weigh you to your pain, are all motivated.

The wind passes the statue
of the dead Man across the square,
stokes the fires in your little body
beside the window, as your room
runs away from you like a whimsical clock,
the beautiful stranger's face
turning about your impedections
as a troubled leaf about its stem:
the escape you would invoke
eating away the moon
that simply exploits the eagerness of the blood.

# The Hour from the Window

These days which always try to stop me,
the glass that swaggers over
my memories, inflaming vein and muscle and glance,
I catch what it is, as I go by, this old voice,

but what is its reason for rising up the night,
this grimness which follows me without a word,
as though it wanted us to meet and yet was afraid,
the footstep behind, the moment that reaches out
for people, and that opens a door.

Maybe I should not believe myself
through all the ideas which have long filled my head,
wondering at the instant, which
with its single cryptic knock,
separates me suddenly, more than death,

from the golden light that turns upon my name:
perhaps the conscience I feared had found its stance,
as under it my ears hear the silence in a sleeper's room,
working away its darkness on a face he did not piece.

■

# The Left Side of Life

This life it cherishes grief.
Eyes that cannot see, the festival
when at last the curtain falls,
the bluish weariness of the sky,
the friendless kick of the blood-ball.
The heart can shut itself off
at a knock at the door, but order
doesn't cease, and dream coalesces
into the sentence of the closed carbon ring.
This life, with the distant cry breaking free
from a fairy-tale tower, passes by
without thought, without breath;
and here, where I laugh myself sick,
was it the real world of the aimless traveler,
looking for resemblances and animal fears
when I was moving away
from my impersonal sense of happiness?

Perhaps talking to myself is an answer,
when I find I'm suddenly not there;
the climate of loss is awful,
and looking up might
show the stars in their magnificence,
though a fog hangs on day and night,
 and the starlight is meaningless because
it is not enough to find each other again.

This life. Will it help to pluck innocence
from the wind that threads our days
and force life out of its cage through a back door?
It's not time that gives life its humanity
but a Gulliver of squandered innocence, so at ease
to isolate the grinning face
and destroy its surrounding silver trails.

# The Morning of the Dead Fish

Cold eyes at the road and through the trees,
beyond their uneven sunrise
where the water softens from its hardness
and folds neatly over the ends of the sky

into pillows of time that hang in place
in the darkened air of this ancient cave.
The same road passing under those fish
whose eyes can rise to the level of the stars,

and whose living eyes charge fierce meaning
in the possession of an unseeing time
that makes a palimpsest in the others' eyes.
For they are the dead, the phantom fish:

with the freshness from a stopped sunrise
they feign a night where no stars shine,
scooping out a moment of strange power
from the deep fields of wild water

that hide the sleek cunning of the game.
For did they merely feign, knowing fully well
how wrong it was, by letting in
the music of rain among peacocks,
to tell the ones who whirled by that their turn would come?

There lies a narrow channel
between the treacherous rock and the fast current;
as here sometimes a quickening is born
like the cryptic crack in some block of wood

which drifts wearily from one state to another.
But it serves no purpose, this quick wake of intuition,
hidden away even in the first morning of love:
simply a lapping of little waves which go nowhere.

Enough to wait, in the cave's thin air,
their scales knotted loose like promises already over,
the dance of the peacocks moving toward them
along the shadowy road of the dream-bound trees,

for no one regains either the whiteness
or the dark, neither these dead nor the living;
but the sunrise, all its terror and despair,
like a lure tumbling across only to the crippled minnow.

■

# The Plot

Yesterday I looked at the bed in my room
and suddenly thought of a victor standing alone
in a battlefield  with empty hands.
Like the horizon, any feeling like this is always
a blur between what's real and what's not.

My life is something else; it's made up of
silences that say more than was safe for one.
And discourses that consume themselves all the time
trying restlessly to keep up with the past.
And prayers that are swallowed by their own griefs.

How can the afternoon hold us
like a keening hymn in the dark wounded fields
we keep pressed between our palms?
How can the hatred  of men protect us from ourselves?
My mind is slow to look under  the clods
of upturned earth, and blind to reject my death.

The colors of the sky have been shamed by the shadows
of my land. My life is something else.
How can I live with the birds who cannot sing
and with the wind that had lost its voice.

staring simply at the fabulous sacred lamps
that perform their ritual in life's musty depths?

Their light makes no sense to me
like a scene from a film that switches
to a language I have not heard until now.
Has the god ruling my life suddenly forgotten its plot?

■

# The Quality of Ruins

Let not the words fill you with fear,
those that trap you like an animal in your heart.
Those that claim you like insects of the night
      in their fiery lighf s path,
those that run down from the snowcapped mountains
      along interminable distances,
those that contort themselves to tangled rivers
      of permanent aloneness,
those that blind you with your own impotence
      and then crush you with the desire
to make things right in the world.

No words are promises, even
the yielding gentleness of the floating breaths
      of dead souls that pull your head down
to rest softly on the breeze;
those so quiet you can hear
the sigh of the waves and the gulls in your soul,
those that cry out from the shores of unspoken pacts,

those that laugh up at you from the bottom of your
      girls lips,
those that appear to release you from the past
that is simply another word, the remains of living,
those of a father that devour you with terror
      at the feeling of bringing perfectness to your life.

And if the words touch your arm restfully in speaking to you
assuring you a future you begin to believe in,
a softening of your body, memory and breath,
so that you turn inward, finding fault
        with everything about yourself,
let it not lead you to the vacant look of martyrdom.
Words have value only if one is not alone,
when you are seated on a golden throne
balanced on your authentic family, trusted friends, children,
and the country from which you cannot cut yourself loose.
The perhaps,
the fabulous road is laid out in front of you,
decked with words, the salient light
        of your own initiated consciousness, a flight
you would follow with joy.

Yet I only know,
this word which lets me survive inside,
this liberal ethic,
is one long error of inexperience.
Who am I to play God with good intentions?
The life closes with the lessons of justice,
good deeds, the arcades of peace;
if the word exists to the end of thought
it is a compromise,
of a symbol ultimately beside,
the cry of a whole clan of people on my back
the fast-talking men and women inside of me
        who fall silent all of a sudden
when a young man approaches them, my son,
        my nephew;
the words my father played, my father's father,
the shaven priest, the government minister:

metallic clicks of the words
resounding  through  the  country of my mind,
those which could commit murder
        in the name of mercy.

My grief
is to endure the words of the living,
those men
who become more distant  every day,
whose bodies and minds have been torn apart
        and face one another  now,
indecently. like old ruins.

# The Season of the Old Rain

This is the season  of the  old rain,
always with much to answer  before  time is done
with  decay  and  death  and  shutting  our minds
to the  jasmine's reason that  keeps growing
in backyards on the edge of water. Here is the bamboo
dropping  beads of twilight on earth's  stricken floor;
bent  and  outstretched, gesturing  gloomily into a gray sky.
This is the time when  the fruit  of my life
seems humble  and  tender  against  the  dark banyan,
when the season comes alive with memories of earlier years.
And when  one's hand,  suddenly  lightened
from the weight of elusive beauty, is almost ready
to  touch  another's.  One knows now
how the moon has tricked the mind, surrounded
by the loves one has slowly grown old with.
Traveler,  where  is it you belong?
Perhaps  watching  the old woman marooned  on a treetop
hemmed in by a wild layer of water called death,
the unseen touches me with one of its
lonely wet winds, unearthing a vein of life.
Perhaps  here in her  eyes the  rebellious  season
held  an  answer  to whatever  I sought,
having  walked  up to the  place that  grew darker
against  torn  homes  and  flattened  hearths
and where the sunset threw up its bloodied  hands.

Once  I remember  I turned  to death
as symbol of my age's memory, and the rain
was green on the grass that chose me my palimpsest
not to learn. And now, it carries one away,
the seen miracle in those eyes, closing and  opening,
revealing neither sorrow nor hope nor loss
and cutting down the fruit of my silent season.

# The Shadow of Day

The bright day winced at my step. Where
was it I could go? The doors were shut,
the parties over, something hung over us
like a cloud that will not bring rain.
Embarrassed, I looked around
for ripe fruit in the bowl.

It was an ordinary day: cut flowers in the vase,
the Leader on the television, the stained mirror
that seemed to forgive me evil, and
Sunday lotuses that betrayed the hour
when they began to bloom. And everyone calm,
following the old proverbs meekly into the world.

For an instant I wondered whether the ethereal
voices of flutes had died out,
whether I had any choice
when I put my arms around you,
almost by instinct; or only to conjure up
over and over again, the crust of days set aside

was one of only lying to oneself when one pretends
one was doing something one did not like?
What I find now is no more
a monstrous secret between us; they are asleep,
and I will repeat my words, getting them wrong again,
filling my tongue and mouth with the swift shadow of day.

# The Shore

At times the boatman
fears someone would push his craft
and force him to cross the river.
Egrets surge past,
monks wearing the same gray cassocks.

Sometimes I am incapable of love.
But the boat is already in midriver,
just the way it is in a dream,
the creak of the puntpole
carrying across our forebodings.

This shore keeps me thinking
why that old road seems to lead here again,
why the current turns me
toward the mystery of the bank.
One night I stood there as a child
terrified by the almost inaudible beat
of the boat tied to the shore;
the truth was more than I could bear.

At times I am afraid
I know more than I should.
Of the dead leaf, its life secretly clenched.
Of the one river to cross, encountered again

and again, apprehended, understood,
then forgotten, lost, and found again.
Not of the simple truth that was itself a metaphor,
with people waiting to be ferried across,
the shadows of our knowledge
condemned to wander the deserted shore.

If I seek an answer to my life,
it's because I see myself everywhere, all the time.
But there is the hard old boatman
watching over the utter desert of his waters.
The river flows without form, intangible.
And when I stand on the shore that is not.

■

# The Skies of Night

Sometimes there is this night,
a sudden sound wakening me from my reverie.
It is speaking my name maybe,
proclaiming something before the final hours,
a moonlight which raves as a delirious child
or some stubborn black root
screaming out of a cracked wall of memories.

It is as though something lies ahead of me,
a grave task I have to perform,
that lures my blood to war.
Or does the sharp blade of time I hold
turn in my bewildered hand?
What sound is it, growing from within,
that feels the false quiet of repose?

I know I am powerless to reveal myself.
Nor do I know how to hold my silence.
Perhaps the voice which returns at nightfall
and lies sleepless with me in my bed
knows it is too late to talk of peace.
My cries merely slide down its walls.
The lies give way beneath me.

# The Trail of Poetry

If solitude, or fear, or pain, or grief
Should be thy portion, with what healing thoughts
Of tender joy wilt thou remember me,
And these my exhortations!

-Wordsworth

Not a souvenir in a shop window,
that you would love it.
Nurture it up from its diapers,
for it to become a man.
For poetry the world lives far away,
among machines, construction sites, boardrooms.
Let it raise you right where you belong.
Sit by the window, looking over the courtyard
into the street. Watch the old pregnant woman
sweeping the litter turn the knot of pain
inside you into a mop to soak up your tears.
Shut yourself up in the jasmine of darkness.
You are one of those who can't go on,
but that's no reason for jumping off
a deserted bridge. Hear the last laugh of horror
of the paralytic who pulls himself up at sunrise
to swallow the bottle of insecticide.
But don't let poetry cauterize you like acid.

Don't  let your life leave
its hiding  place to search for a weapon
in order to protect yourself from life itself,
which refuses all the doors to open.
You have to check whether  poetry
really becomes  a cry for protecting man.
It is always  a very unequal fight.
You would  know  many  things,
but perhaps not know those certainties
from which some other worldly manifestation
must take its role.
The blue-eyed  metaphor,  for instance.
Does it make our desires ridiculous
in its final order, the sublime stone
that speaks no bond and no farewell?
That it might be impassioned as death
which allows one to survive-or possess
the lonely day of fireflies with the flash of light?
There is nothing to tell, you think,
after making your march home with your stories,
letting  poetry step on your feelings.
That you threw stones at birds or little animals,
that your childhood shook beneath their feet,
the yearning for provocation,
your dead father's ash that forced out of you a word;
the persistent nightmare  isn't poetry.
You are certainly not mute,
but silence is because of poetry.
So go naked into the immoral world of clothes.
The night  justifies the sorrow
of the warm lighted windows along the streets.
The cemetery  sparkles for a while
from the proud  mouths of its funerals.

When things are serious, cast your own life
from another's real life by the lost wax of hope.
Answer the possibilities. And do not say:
This heart is silent. It has no voice.
It has spent its day in nakedness, raising Cain.
There is not even a farewell on which to stand.
That the words have lost their coordinates.
Simply that the words make you believe
you stand at the end of the world
where you can scarcely find the way back to yourself.

■

# Things that Happen

A new light lays open things.
It alone has moved as I watch.
Here I'd like to make myself presentable to please
this other, and as I stroke the rain off my hair,
the earth of the garden cracks to let out the dark.
For years my body has lied, simply because through it
lies the way, the way ripeness comes to warm
the hand of the season that trained it.

To become myself, it is not possible that
it will be taken away from me, all that I loved.
Would it be in the color on my face, as it passes
to the face of the person I have just met and shared?
Old sunsets move again in my sky
without amazing me. With this feeling
that everything has a beginning and an end.

Around me are people, hurrying about;
the guns on the mountains, ominously silent;
the words of freedom locked in the day's newspapers.
This other pace threatens my sweet lies
and plotted resistance to my fears.
The bull ambling down the street can
still be seen from here, like yesterday.
And the same woman, looking out for the real moon

in her child's notebook. The small promises, too,
blown away quickly by another's breath.

But those things that happen
have always beginnings that cannot be seen.
have always beginnings that cannot be seen.

It is the body I think I've carried all along,
forcing me to wander  from secret
to secret, mirage to mirage,
pumping up half-truths into a reality I never lived.

Something in the light withers me into a shadow
of myself. I begin to make foolish demands
to ward off the fine rain of fear.
This time is a fish out of water.
And our bodies bear the old marks of its thrashings.

■

# Unreal Country

Rain grates in the silence. My son
walks in through the dim walls,
a strange map drawn by life.

It's as though, blind,
one goes on feeling for night.
And a lot of space I touch

that turns grandly into darkness.
His lost face, white enamel,
looks down at his feet

as if to say: Only the world
is left, and the rain
that hangs from the branches.

Searching for stars still, he asks:
What haven't you told me yet?
And through the dull suburbs

of his death, my old father
gropes his way back.
Yes, he seems to whisper,

overwhelmed by the defeat
in my eyes, hunger and earth
made the bones of one's breath.

I see them nod to each other,
suddenly in fear of the rain,
of the heart left behind.

# Waiting

Balanced on a ball of reverent light,
under your feet the deadened dust,
you hardly allow yourself the right
to die any other kind of death.
The smell of age sticks to you innocently
You shift years noiselessly in your eyes.

There on the eminence of the sun
five-thousand-year  ribs shine cruelly,
soiled three-year-old children
looking for healing their burnt  veins of air.
You hardly know the vision isolates you, the real,
you are reduced to stone,

not yourself. Who are you, the one
that stares at you from far off,
the one you are not going to die with?
Does the brood of white-clad
luckless widows shuffling up and down
the fractured  temple steps distress you?

Every day I see them debase themselves
and am afraid, understanding nothing, the entire land
immobile, like the River in its used infirm bed.
The bodiless voices of priests are like quicksands,
waiting for your apprehensions  to enter them.
The death that comes swings back and forth
like a bewitched  barge upon a weaker race.

# Wandering into Each Other

We don't know what we are, what youth is.
Unlike us, youths never like to wait
with the happiness they feel they have.
Our taste reeks of sacrifice.

Embarrassing, our stories
run out of our days and face us later
with the bleached skulls strewn
across the city's cremation grounds.

Life doesn't give us a day off.
I know now what my father thought:
he lay dying in front of us and all our care
was simply pretense.
What is it that continues to pace the room?
Whatever it is, the young will only know
how to smother it in their arms. We'll simply
stand beside it, you and I, afraid
to lose control, because
we think we were dreaming this.
*They* know, affiicted both with its terror
and desire. Out of our minds for happiness,
I hold out my hand for you to take it:
its skin scarred with wounds from being caught
in its own cunningly laid snares.

# Woman in Love

This earth,
strange shore of strength,
to touch you with its wand of lasting power.
Into your silence of sacred tree-shadows
hails the trumpet  of the sun: a madness
of birds, chirpy chantings of flight,
song of tropic fire.

Warmth,  the lavender  glow of light,
settles happily in the dark dreams
of your blessing of the tawny breasts
that swell below those white shoulders
of sleep. In your magic harvest
the birds  of your  breath  dance
and tremble the soft darkness
of your womb with desire.
And each vein answers with lucent wonder

Woman, what things
you would  make me remember,
what would you make me do?
Which night shall sweep across
the dark sky of sleep and come down
to rest in the  jonquil field of day?
Which farewell or departure
won't wait for the silence
to grow easily into the  pain of our bodies?

Childhood, virginal,
as if adrift
in the river of sunlight you carry inside you,
as the water sobs through the tangled rocks
          of relationship,
that makes one
as though leaving a place of crime.
As earth goes on
to conquer us with blind windows of grief,
and blood makes us feel so small.

And if on the endless blue waves of your body
someone leaves a boat, a touch,
it would only drift about, like a child asleep,
tired after the day,
the wondering expression on its face
wandering against the inattentive waves,
while perhaps your soul,
like the tide, along the endless drift of seaweed,
faces its How in the dark,
a flow blissfully unaware
what rocks of power it holds outside of it.

# A Mood of Denial

If you feel you are alone,
there must be a shadow inside you.
This shadow must have come
from the past you did not want to be in.
And if you are going out the door,
you don't know if it's the same
person you are when you come back in.

It's always wise not to think
what is outside the door:
the wings with enough sky to last
a lifetime, and the loneliness
that melts into thin air inside
the white envelope in your hands.

But your past says you're never alone.
The life inside goes on without you,
disconnected electrical wires leading nowhere,
with your shadow that detects death
before you know where you are.
You will never find out any trace
of the silent dialogue it has been
carrying on while you were blinded
by the light of unexplained excitement.

Perhaps the shadow can only save you
from the memory of the past.
And if you feel you are alone
because of your misunderstanding with life,
your shadow will go on treating you
as though you are already condemned.

Life, you would think then,
is a stupid wind that has lost its wings.
And if you open your past enough
to see into your own shadow,
you all but become the shadow itself.

# A Poem at Fifty-One

I sit here waiting for her, sit here
with the empty skin drooping over my shoulders
as I had already sat waiting many times before
beside the same window, in the same old chair.
Once in a while, I'd open my notebooks,
find the words I had written float away
into the wilderness on the other side of the paper
like the smoke drifting over the burning-ground
of my own flesh. I shut my tired eyes.
And I try not to think of the quick warm skin
of the eighteen-year-old girl I met last month.
I stretch my lonely lips into an unforgivable grin.
I turn my face over in the darkness of my room
and peer into it; but I don't remember now
when my beard had started to grow.
I let the minute drop the hour to the ground;
but each time it came back, and I had to do this
all over again, to put the mind at ease.
I touch my shoulders; they are bare, contrite,
like the shape of a deserted park bench in the rain.
Was some sort of change coming over me?
Or was it time's empty skin, waiting for an excuse
to advance the blood, to keep it occupied?
My notebooks are there, my pretty wife too,
but I have been with them too long, long in love,

and they have worn me slowly around the edges.
Or maybe it isn't because of them, themselves;
it's because of where I came from, and of what
I realized suddenly I was really waiting for:
the life that my life seeks, when I go in
to answer it, but it had gone the other way
to where I couldn't meet it at all,
as I go back to where I was, by the same window,
without a word, waiting for her,
empty skin flapping like truce flags in a losing war.

# A Spring Morning

Morning's clear light. At a naked window,
my hands  spread  on the broad  sill,
the joy I feel is real as the flowers' promise
all over my body's cage.

Beyond, sunlight keeps falling on
the narrow feathered backs of birds;
they are the little friends  in the right places.
And I was a tree then,  and  the branches
held  that moment no human being could reach.

Tender ferns open  their  eyes,
coils of dreamlike light move my feet,
the gentle  embrace of the world is entrapped
in my full morning cup of the sky.

It does not matter  today if the light
has spent  its night  in another's arms.
It's here  with me now, with a story
of a million words. Great glittering wings
of light, and  the longing in your eyes.

From each flower rises a susurrus  of wings.
And each  touch  is never away
from  the certain  feeling  that there  would be
time in abundance to cross the empty space
of midnight and  hold  the shape  of love.

# Afterward

Outside, the silence of another night
waits for the whine of the crickets.
Somewhere along the rim of this tired valley
a star called Sirius shines madly,
a little tide rises and falls,
naked in death.

The music has gone, days of words
won't let this body escape.
A destiny loosens
in the meaningless sounds of waves
and the hissing of strange wood fires.

Voices of others cover my eyes,
the benevolence of time along railway tracks
you travelled once.
Go nearer yourself, my child,
so you can recognize Time.

Something like light
begins to risk the sullen darkness.
If I were to say a prayer,
it would only be another language
on my tongue, a tiny shape of light
waiting to touch the water of the sea.

■

# Again the Rain Falls

Again the rain falls on my earth
without a murmur,
where mute waterfalls bleed
over the years of my youth.

The last flight of winter cranes
has taken time away
as an answer. Only
voices of the dead filter down the stairs.

My room is bare, and outside
the young bamboos bend into the wind
and the rain turns in silence.
A young man who resembles my son

is out there in thought, in open green,
planning his own garden.
Rain stands on the margins of my time,
a discovery, like theft.

making me careful how I lay the hour down,
looking at the trees growing too large
for my little yard, filling with lurid light,
and I hardly see spring coming in.

■

# An Abandoned Temple, Orissa

An intriguing weariness perhaps,
or some dark story from our hunger
drifts from the fraying walls
to think its thousand thoughts
among the slumped, coarse trees.
Silence had not closed its mouth still,
or buried its featureless pilgrimage.
Perhaps time had simply pulled its head
in between its shoulders and pressed itself
against the unfeeling stone of its own design.

The lostness talks. A pipal
had sheered into one of the grimacing walls, a final
agony for a soul never wasted,
like time. If the temple could
crawl up the field waving its arms drunk
with the feeling of loss, would a place of magic know
whether to drown itself or go on living?
When your heart comes crawling on all fours, what use
is there covering your mouth
with your innocent handfuls of life?

The temple meets me, everlasting grass on graves. Was
there a world beyond
I had never paused to consider?
I open my eyes and see nothing, as I go on to build the
darkness of the spirit
into a houseless, noiseless city which never exists;
as though trying to carry our pain or madness into the
air of a strange surrender
that holds back any awareness of grief.

# Ann

This summer is as bare as the last one
had been. Fires lurk in the hills beyond the river,
mocking the empty altar in my neighbour's house
and the lost hour of vows. Pale pigeons flying
in silence; and a lemon rain-tree flower drifts
carrying its crown of farewell. A silence
that makes me invoke your name again: "Ann?"
May winds flog the trees, and the murmur of your voice
passes by the vacant swings under the peepuls
that fail to awake from dreams in which they live.
What makes one suffer the thought
that silence owns the mind? The present
which memory will not enable us to live in?
Meaninglessly I reach for someone's hand.
For as we move from one hour to another
I know I'll be here again before summer is scarcely gone.
Unconcerned I watch a stone fragment from a ruined temple
being set up ceremoniously on a pedestal,
into quiet wonder, a deity;
and I hear the stir of the wind among the dead leaves
on my heart's ground as the evening's first star appears,
springing out of the flames of the burning ground beyond,
a faint flower of ash: "Ann?"

# Another Autumn

The south wind blows steadily from the river,
overtakes me in a fancy of flight;
it startles the ashes of the dead
on the riverbank, flutters the thin maps
in the map seller's hand, it presses open
the gleaming canopies of the festival,
and gasps among the old, mossed stones. From here
I can see the wind moving the bracken,
moving so fiercely that it blurs all thought,
tracks of a season. And this my room
which preserves each ulterior motive,
my notebooks and radio signals I presume upon;
where my feet easily slip into and out of my shoes
but where the wind can speak no farther
and be a measure of an aroma
that once held a flower's soul.

Here, while everything stands still
to make me tremble to old post cards I received once,
I watch myself looking out of the window
at a fallen branch, from my room, past the map seller,
toward someone who could call out my name
and come in, to drown me again
in those songs of pain and loss, to make me cry
like my father's child, and find

ultimately that thoughtless corner where moss waits
patiently to appear
in the cracks of a dream's walls.
But I can hear no song now, feeling
my eyelids close, as the wind comes and goes;
as hair thins and hardens,
and emptiness echoes from the ashes of truth;
as wind, map and river are swallowed
by the trajectories of daylight,
and my need to have you is only caught
in the design for a poem I have been working on.

Autumn is here again, my hand trembles
to the wind, but you are not responsible,
you are not what you seem;
like an unknown horoscope which pushes one
against a wall, absent lover-
perhaps only a fear of some memory
that has no further use for gentleness or remorse,
as the wind elsewhere
nudges your yearning skin with long cool fingers.

■

# At Times an Unknown Star

At times an unknown star falls down
the edge of the ravine, pretending innocence,
and something reminds me that pain began
when my father led me into those lands
where laws have never been broken.
I am somewhere else today, the television
is on; and history, that undiscovered country
I'd once thought it to be, only pushed me
into childhood where we learnt
to spread our arms wide for love and honor.

Almost everyone talks the same way about love:
they say there is this time that humbles one
as if one were that empty corner of the street
meant for the day's litter, when the heart
can't believe it is hiding, startling it
into a thousand starlings, flying through
the light, rousing others to flight.
I'd begin to believe my country was different,
that poetry and science and religion
walk still the same road; they could deceive;
that the clutch in the throat is made
of moonlight and rushes in the shallows of the river.

Down the street a water faucet is open,
gushing into the gutter. Another star falls
as I wait, and the time inside me rises
to the edge of my life like long shadows falling
across the grass that has lost its green.

Bulbuls begin to sing from nearby trees once again;
like many others I realize I live
for just one such moment, when pain
with its invisible mouth closes around the rim
of my glass, and I stare at this bared heart,
a clown in a circus with his perpetual smile.

# Dust

It's dust, colouring those secret horizons
of the bone day after day,
true prophet of life's sunset.
A blood-red silence flows into my eyes.

It's absurd to be afraid.
Of the anonymous rush of redness,
and the sudden understanding
that this blindness exists just here, and now-

the blindness of turning away
from the all-knowing horizon, heavy
with the triumph of memory, when
the heart is trapped in a clutch of light.

But what astonishes me most
is that I know dust is my hidden child,
in waking and in sleep,
a lonely idol whom only faith can shield;
as the softness of meteors of ancient spirits
comes sifting down through the blindfold of my fears.

# A Mood of Denial

If you feel you are alone,
there must be a shadow inside you.
This shadow must have come
from the past you did not want to be in.
And if you are going out the door,
you don't know if it's the same
person you are when you come back in.

It's always wise not to think
what is outside the door:
the wings with enough sky to last
a lifetime, and the loneliness
that melts into thin air inside
the white envelope in your hands.

But your past says you're never alone.
The life inside goes on without you,
disconnected electrical wires leading nowhere,
with your shadow that detects death
before you know where you are.
You will never find out any trace
of the silent dialogue it has been
carrying on while you were blinded
by the light of unexplained excitement.

Perhaps the shadow can only save you
from the memory of the past.
And if you feel you are alone
because of your misunderstanding with life,
your shadow will go on treating you
as though you are already condemned.

Life, you would think then,
is a stupid wind that has lost its wings.
And if you open your past enough
to see into your own shadow,
you all but become the shadow itself.

# A Poem at Fifty-One

I sit here waiting for her, sit here
with the empty skin drooping over my shoulders
as I had already sat waiting many times before
beside the same window, in the same old chair.
Once in a while, I'd open my notebooks,
find the words I had written float away
into the wilderness on the other side of the paper
like the smoke drifting over the burning-ground
of my own flesh. I shut my tired eyes.
And I try not to think of the quick warm skin
of the eighteen-year-old girl I met last month.
I stretch my lonely lips into an unforgivable grin.
I turn my face over in the darkness of my room
and peer into it; but I don't remember now
when my beard had started to grow.
I let the minute drop the hour to the ground;
but each time it came back, and I had to do this
all over again, to put the mind at ease.
I touch my shoulders; they are bare, contrite,
like the shape of a deserted park bench in the rain.
Was some sort of change coming over me?
Or was it time's empty skin, waiting for an excuse
to advance the blood, to keep it occupied?
My notebooks are there, my pretty wife too,
but I have been with them too long, long in love,

and they have worn me slowly around the edges.
Or maybe it isn't because of them, themselves;
it's because of where I came from, and of what
I realized suddenly I was really waiting for:
the life that my life seeks, when I go in
to answer it, but it had gone the other way
to where I couldn't meet it at all,
as I go back to where I was, by the same window,
without a word, waiting for her,
empty skin flapping like truce flags in a losing war.

■

# A Spring Morning

Morning's clear light. At a naked window,
my hands  spread  on the broad  sill,
the joy I feel is real as the flowers' promise
all over my body's cage.

Beyond, sunlight keeps falling on
the narrow feathered backs of birds;
they are the little friends  in the right places.
And I was a tree then,  and  the branches
held  that moment no human being could  reach.

Tender ferns open  their  eyes,
coils of dreamlike light move my feet,
the gentle  embrace of the world is entrapped
in my full morning cup of the sky.

It does not matter  today if the light
has spent  its night  in another's arms.
It's here  with me now, with a story
of a million words. Great glittering wings
of light, and  the longing in your eyes.

From each flower rises a susurrus  of wings.
And each  touch  is never away
from  the certain  feeling  that there  would be
time in abundance to cross the empty space
of midnight and  hold  the shape  of love.

# Afterward

Outside, the silence of another night
waits for the whine of the crickets.
Somewhere along the rim of this tired valley
a star called Sirius shines madly,
a little tide rises and falls,
naked in death.

The music has gone, days of words
won't let this body escape.
A destiny loosens
in the meaningless sounds of waves
and the hissing of strange wood fires.

Voices of others cover my eyes,
the benevolence of time along railway tracks
you travelled once.
Go nearer yourself, my child,
so you can recognize Time.

Something like light
begins to risk the sullen darkness.
If I were to say a prayer,
it would only be another language
on my tongue, a tiny shape of light
waiting to touch the water of the sea.

# Again the Rain Falls

Again the rain falls on my earth
without a murmur,
where mute waterfalls bleed
over the years of my youth.

The last flight of winter cranes
has taken time away
as an answer. Only
voices of the dead filter down the stairs.

My room is bare, and outside
the young bamboos bend into the wind
and the rain turns in silence.
A young man who resembles my son

is out there in thought, in open green,
planning his own garden.
Rain stands on the margins of my time,
a discovery, like theft,

making me careful how I lay the hour down,
looking at the trees growing too large
for my little yard, filling with lurid light,
and I hardly see spring coming in.

■

# An Abandoned Temple, Orissa

An intriguing weariness perhaps,
or some dark story from our hunger
drifts from the fraying walls
to think its thousand thoughts
among the slumped, coarse trees.
Silence had not closed its mouth still,
or buried its featureless pilgrimage.
Perhaps time had simply pulled its head
in between its shoulders and pressed itself
against the unfeeling stone of its own design.

The lostness talks. A pipal
had sheered into one of the grimacing walls,
a final agony for a soul never wasted,
like time. If the temple could
crawl up the field waving its arms drunk
with the feeling of loss, would a place of magic
know whether to drown itself or go on living?
When your heart comes crawling on all fours,
what use is there covering your mouth
with your innocent handfuls of life?

The temple meets me,
everlasting grass on graves.
Was there a world beyond
I had never paused to consider?
I open my eyes and see nothing, as I go on
to build the darkness of the spirit
into a houseless, noiseless city which never exists;
as though trying to carry our pain or madness
into the air of a strange surrender
that holds back any awareness of grief.

# Father

My old father believes, even in his last days;
that is why he isn't a lover or a poet.
He cannot drown himself in water. Or in awe.
And the cicadas throb in the haze of the hours,
and our lives do not allow us
to see into their hearts
or to interpret their silence when they've ceased to be.

But that is how it is to be left behind,
when dreams of the dying
breathe in the rising of the sun,
and they smell of life-
as I shut the bedroom door softly
and he raises his heavy-lidded eyes, drops them
and asks: "What am I doing here with you?"

A deep wrinkle of the light closes my eyes.
Above is the sky and stars lie in it.

■

# Guavas

It's the guavas. Hanging up there,
warm, earthy, the rouse of remembered passion.
Watching them, my mind doesn't bend
to deny I'm not able to feel anything,
as I begin to hear again the weapons
that waken death in the world. Today,
if I'm not running away from lifeless life,
I try to enter a city where people
made me see myself as a nightmare
which didn't approve of sanctions and fear.

Elsewhere, men plunder and kill. Someone
speaks of a lonely village wife who wanders
from one night of rape to another, wanting
only to survive in her children.
I breathe deeply of this air of habit,
the air of guavas whose green only moves
from the sensuousness of a cage to cage.
Unlike them I wish I wouldn't have to fight,
feel the wild throb of forgotten lust,
rearrange those dead of mine who had killed
themselves or died of penury or heart attacks
until they awakened again, blessed,
and not feel the spasms of fear I express.

Today it's of no use to find whether
the game we're in denies us or not.
Truth is never caught by the dry and ugly
governments which do not change.
When I awake on this particular morning,
I have no idea I could court danger
for a cause I only half understand.

A green which can make me hide my own nature
still goes on feasting on the innocences
of childhood, watching me; the endless bags
under their eyes trembling sadly
to the wind whistling past our years.

■

# Letting in the Darkness

It wasn't another world yet.
Words failed me.
Father's face had darkened
as he lay there;
the laughter of brash  prostitutes
against his face
made  me feel embarrassed, restless.
Pain said nothing again.
The  trees beyond  swayed
in the warm, moist-earth wind.
If a dream  would hold one captive,
one could forgive everything,
detach  oneself from  the life he lived.
Madness can withhold  secret  fantasies.
But this wasn't another world yet.
Father  didn't want to escape
his ravaged, vacant landscape.
He breathed deeply,
staring  at the arm of the chair
that was still full of the sadness
left over from a vibrant life.
But when a gecko scurried across
a wall, a tremor came over him
as though a last ritual
to wake up the dead
sounded keenly in his ears.
My voice, pointlessly it seemed,

only whipped up mud on the path.
Wearing  clothes was indecent
when everyone  else was naked.
This world returned
from its aimless wandering
and stretched out its vague hope
that his grandmother would
catch up with him by dawn.
Had  he learnt to overcome his fear
before  he climbed  the mountain?
When  would he know of the door
which he never knew existed
that  had opened within him?
Banal and wordless,
it has never answered  me,
reminding me of aging women
with lonely longing eyes.
I look at Father's small, poor  mouth
and  there,
was my world in his,
one world at the other world.
I saw the rivers flow past
where fathers  drown  themselves.
How was one  to go along
the road and  the hunger?
The  house sighed.
For a breathless second
something resembling Father's love
brushed  past me,
untouchable and  mysterious.
The  door  had opened and shut,
glazed with moonlight, cold.

# Limping from an Old Wound

Instead of wearing
the clouds around its neck,
the sky has pushed them into its wounds.
Hawks are beautiful in violence
even when they swoop to kill.

Rain buries its face in my hands,
not knowing what to do.
Its unbearable redness
begins to weep in silence.
There are these shadows which can
only stand beside the sighing sal trees.

When the sun leaves, tired of its light,
and road and landscape stop unwinding
in the distance,
the poet reaches just for a sorrow
shadows that have no size or shape
can only bring.

# Of this Evening

This evening I look at that part of myself
which remains with me, but I do not know
what it is, hard to recognize it any more.
I don't think I can reach it when I want it so much.
Is it because my years have had a lot of weight
on them, or because the world has come to know
what I already know about that part of me?
A curtain rises slowly upon a stage
with nothing to reveal, no scene or spell or time.
And what remains with me is a tricky weapon,
difficult to use. It is not that I face
a total stranger suddenly sometimes,
like some wide door barred in rosewood and iron;
or that I hold that part responsible
for making me grovel in front of the world
that beats around me like my ambitious heart.
Days still pretend to belong;
they see me struggling to push them away
but I seem to have no strength left,
perhaps I shall follow quietly after them.
This evening a part of myself closes in on me,
the room is awfully quiet and empty;
but I can hear the shame and pain of defeat
playing mercilessly about my shoulders,
the key lost, and that part trying to pry
my longing away which sits silent like
a grey owl on a branch of my breath,
eyes wide open in another dumb, dirty trick.

# Rain

The scent of black soil.
Slush on the canal banks,
along the shacks
sluggishly pressed against each other.
Nobody talks about the world outside.

Beyond the darkness
the fiercely rising river.
No stars shiver in it.
A glowworm, generous in its light,
flies me into darkness.

From some doorway
small notes of a song slip by.
It's a pulse beat,
bringing in a memory, a road
or lie for one to carry on,
or a something that allows me
to be part of who they are.

Bicycle bells slow down
the rain's drowsy fall.
The cool night air seems real.
Somewhere, someone
is at a summer story once again,
with words that only work
in the real world, where
we live on without knowing.

■

# Rice[1]

Crumpled old villages,
overgrown with skin and flesh.
Inane faces of stone lions
stare on from torn temple entrances.

Memory carries me into strange lands,
my arm around the iron shoulders
of desolate paddy fields.
History, dead river, torments me.
Like the weak, the gods too held back,
accepting their lot,
as the crickets scraped, meaningless.

Here the sleepless nights of summer
simply come and go.
The rice has lost its wings;
it does not tremble in the wind.
Each waking takes all day to cool down.
Because I have lived within stories,
even when I've loved someone
or sat down to write another futile poem.
But did the world believe in
an exhausted fairy tale,
when innocence was small enough
to fit inside the turnings
of my grandfather's uncertain chemistries,
in that endless night when
he learnt that truth itself was a metaphor?

The indrawn breath;
I've been with it all these years.
And never adulated my own dead.
But at times
a worn-out summer left behind
stumbles against the falling skin
of fallow rice fields
as I feel my way
along the defeating distances of hunger.

■

---

[1] Starving, on the point of death, my grandfather embraced Christianity during the terrible famine that ravaged Orissa in 1866. He was sixteen.

# Signs

Something glances at me over my shoulder.
What does it see?
Old clothes, familiar days, bright instincts,
and those intimate little things that count in the end.
Or does it hear those silent footsteps
that remind one of the hushed noises
of a hundred settled birds at dusk?
Maybe it feels the tight curl of my fingers
in my pocket.
To tell the truth, a voice inside
calls for help still. The childish sorrow
leaps at me like a cat, when I feel
I have become someone else. My life cannot remember
when between the all and the nothing, I found
everything the opposite of what I had imagined.
It recalls how once it watched over
the morals of a nation, looking to an uneasy future.
I drift past prisons, their torture chambers,
and my rage against a distant past.
And drag myself away both from beauty queens
and mangled lepers, the religious grandeur of priests,
fanatical in love with the secret scents of their bodies,
while they risk their keyless farewells.
Memories heavy with weariness,
that serve not as heroes

but hostages that left no room for compromise.
One begins a day by looking at oneself
in the glass. It becomes a challenge,
as if the image, unable to bear its stillness,
didn't know which way to look,
almost losing its perfection and its balance.
Is this a symptom people can't bear to see,
the sign that is able to change them?
That the sudden stillness drags its hunt
back to the mouth of the cave?
Before the hand, out of nowhere,
touches the shoulder?
The strange grief of the blue in the sky
peers down at me. The calmness my father
showed once is a thousand miles away.

■

# The Hour

*After my son's death, March 10, 2018*

Someone looks around for somewhere to go,
when my heart flutters heavily in my chest,
the sick blue tuberose can hardly beat its wings
against the breeze, as old men go out to sit
by themselves, assuming the manners of each other.

This is where the light does not belong to those
passing through, to those who do not belong
in the moments where the light, unable to climb
onto a poem and build itself into the art of death,
lies down righteously in a patch of grass.

Time and the sky roil into signs of night,
the prophet with his scrambled dreams loses himself
in the turns of the world, and squab pigeons
fly free somewhere out there, look down, pushing
through a shadow in the air into another world.

# The Road

It's not  the road anymore
along which my mother sent me on errands.
Nor where dogs slept all day with one eye open,
their tails pestered by flies.
It's not the road which chewed its lip indecisively
waiting for the future to be predicted.
Nor is it the road  that steered me once
into  the heart of one  primeval garden.

The  one I have taken now
appears to fill me with purpose and strength.
But I do not know if it is the happy one.
Even little children walk through its chaos enchanted,
protected by its purposeful air.
Nobody stops them.
Here  I watch them  never lose their way,
their flimsy lightness  building their  delirium.

Eternally  thirsty, the road  has freed  itself
from  the pull of the earth  and  the empty burden
of graves. But its spirit is heavy
with reasons for killing one another.
Something slithers  past as I watch,
from  the garden someone left behind in my heart.
I try to think  of home.
I come  upon  tracks of tall pylons in the dust.

■

# The Wind

The sky darkens. The afternoon wind
drifts through the lanes of this ruined town
and wrecks the images on the placid river
that holds the sudden terror
of a man falling into frigid depths.

My eyes are getting used to the dark.
From time to time
my old father comes at me
with outstretched arms of judgment
and I answer from no clear place I am in.

Beyond, the bare necks of rice
sway in the shadows of Orissa's villages,
the leaves of rain-trees collapse,
and the weak in mind look on helpless
at the afternoons lying bound at their feet,
and at the dark fruit pulling down the trees
of knowledge with their weight-

And now in a dream I hear someone's laughter
and it's no longer the same. In the wind
which carries the ash, the smoke, the odor
which finally settles on the skin
like rain on the funeral grounds of summer;
as the wind twists and turns,
rising like flowers of fierce color out of the ashes,
like dreams strangling the hearts of old men
who feel they were always born old, and the voices
of water inside them come back again and again
as a sound of their dead mothers' weeping.

■

# Uneasy, in the Silent Night

for Runu

Uneasy, here in the silent night.
Blind all along, blind to the real meaning
of death and its life, we come up with a play,
where the actors, with nowhere to turn, simply
palpitate slowly like stars streaming out in the sky.

It's the wounds of your life that look down
at me, uncertain what to do; and your eyes, shut,
leaving, to find another life on another world.
I am the stranger who would hold back his tears,
my spirit conditioned to the actor's body, hard, disciplined.

And I look for the pain when I lean over
your cold face, as I realize I was using it
to escape whatever it was I was running from.
Perhaps memory, helpless against love or sympathy,
hovering above the ground like rain that never fell.

Among the carnival frenzy in Como, that day,
I saw the fear in your eyes, hugging your chest,
your lips ghosting a smile. You are what you are.
Floating against the sides of this day, oh love,
let the silent night make us love the silence of your love.

■

# Village Evening

This evening, fruit bats will hang once again
from the rain-wet deodars
and the wind
tug at the clothes draped
around God's little idol
at the foot of the ageing banyan.
In the dingy air of her hut,
Ahalya, the widow, caresses the rupee
her seven-year-old son
has brought home from his day-long labours,
and dreams of daybreak.
The whole village seems to crouch
in the darkness of faith.
Life hungers in this humid air,
not ashamed of Ahalya's bare voice:
"What a relief there are just
the two of us! Or else
this little money would get us nowhere."
The air flows through the paddy fields, becoming
movement, blood, breath; but stranger
than rape and murder without a scream.
And in the round, indifferent eyes of God,
another shudder passes through the thin body;
as Ahalya, moving sleepily, unrolls her mat,
her promise to feed her son milk-curd next morning
another faraway dream.

■

# A Brief Orissa Winter, 2000

A puddle of fire by the roadside.
Warming hands of passersby.
Elsewhere, a schoolgirl gets ready for class,
flapping her wings like a bird
about to take flight.
Both people who live one or a hundred lives
rinse their bodies with the cool winter air.

No more do men go out onto the earth
to be close enough to the mountain's quiet
and wait for an answer.
No more does anyone who tries to talk of love
defeat death with his certainties.

Already the ash has leapt out of the fire
that lit the darkness of a savage winter night,
and the ground beneath it
is ready once again with its mysteries.
The schoolgirl doesn't want an answer;
she just wants someone to agree with her.
The sun is now low in the sky.
So much science, so my prayer,
and in this darkness that has invaded our lives
a bird whistles by, down the mountain
to where the clouds floated along,
floating past the way they always had.

■

# A Death

A remembered face, a window,
time's lowered eyes:
hunched and trembling, hope survives.

Here, where I live t
he wild weed grows all over the skin.
Like a photographer's light

it strikes hard between the ribs.
And these passive pages of day
go on uttering words

my death urges at the wrong time.
Which is the wisdom I could use?
In deep shadows

a heavy shower traces the path
hidden under the weeds.
The silenced shout of a child

drifts into its mother's arms.
And through the window
the wind bleeds

through cells of unkind laughter,
as I learn to let fall
those words with casual indifference.

# Afternoon Ceremonies

The flatness of the earth beneath our feet
all of a sudden, the wind left behind
in the trees, in between the fingers;
and an afternoon monochrome light
which pushes the blind mind ahead of time.

In all this land
dream is lost like unending railway tracks.
How true that these hands appear
to meet again after months, like two strangers!

All lives are not equal. Who would not
refuse to die this way? Perhaps henceforward
voices from afar will enter the head,
substance of an eternal debris
that cannot be cleared up with desire or pain.

Maybe in dreams it is easy to handle death,
easy to be betrayed by the butterfly
fluttering in search of absent flowers
or by the cry of the wounded dog on the highway
spreading its bare entrails in the sun.
Maybe my dying father is no longer conscious today,
a part of our laughter that gives forth silence.

In this room of mine
last year's calendar hangs uselessly on the wall.
In my mother's eyes pain begins to stir again
like a venerable old gentleman who has returned from afar.

And the sham earth locks us
into a quiet peace park among the world's horrors.
We raise flowers in it. In time to
settle down to afternoon ceremonies.
Cursed from the earth, the wind
wraps white cloths about the flowers' faces:
lost prophets
stirring sluggishly for a god yet to be born.

# Again, One Day, Walking
# by the River

The same river, the same sun, the same town.
Out of the corner of my eye
the barge loaded with golden hay
trapped like a leaf in a basin of water.
A tar drum smolders in front of the judge's house
as four women workers rub the hot tar
onto the pitted face of the road.
It it two in the afternoon and
the heat of yesterday still clings to the old walls
like harsh salt on the skin.
I feel a light wind, so weak and thin
I can't say where it came from.
The day is not yet over. Soon
the mangled lepers will shuffle along, going home,
their helpless looks drawing farttasies on the town square.
I can't remember hearing anyone
saying that he will mourn for me when I am gone.
The tar smoke scatters unnoticed over the water.
I wonder where the day goes.
Even in the bright sun, this was a world I did not know.

# At Times a Man Growing Old

At times a man growing old
plays with a knife
On its edge
the stars shake pitifully

Perhaps he loves this more
than anything  in the world
because it can inflict
severe wounds on time

If he turns  the night darker
and the silence deeper
it's because the wind
doesn't like him touching it
and because the earth  is afraid
at the power of his feeling

A man growing older
is lost in all the forces
he thinks  he knows everything  about
and in all the hungers
that have sucked away his tendernes

It gets lonely
when the rain doesn't wet him
Lonelier too

when he can't find his way out
of this hour
where sleep cannot  reach

Memory's thousand shapes
seek him out:
an old letter
from a girl long gone
is a door
into the world of nightmares

Because he is afraid
of what he wants to bring into bein

And when the man growing old
plucks a flower
he is surprised
at the little darkness
limping out of the bushes

Shadows pass through him

And on the edge of the knife
the bewildered light
merely appears  to frown
at a play of fortune
it doesn't understand

# Cloak of White

When another funeral passes,
the street seems ready
to defend itself once again.
Mana was seven
when she lost her father
and her mother left
to live with another man.
Deaths seem so necessary here
for the calm lassitude
that follows a violent disturbance.
It is human
for death to enter a house,
only then do the rooms
hum their little tunes-
they are not merely spaces
for housing dead things.
My father wanted
to explain the world to me,
he ended up
by talking about the sublime.
He heard nothing more.
He never taught me
to wait for the day to break.
Life, for him, was a betrayal;
through a rain of ash and fire,

through the ignoble thing
that is a man's dream,
through the faces he encountered
in cruel religious posters
and the nakedness of love.
Today I wish
he hadn't died under his own truth,
eating from my hand
as he lay dying,
feeding in resigned silence.
I go out and start walking.
I do not choose a direction.
The world
comes to a conclusion
about everything,
it allows me
to peel the skin off
the face of the dead,
to take hold of a moment
with the passivity of innocence
and draw it out
from its place of concealment,
from where both pain and joy
and the light of suns and distance
can scarcely be distinguished
under their cloak of white.

■

# Crossworlds

Is Japan, this new world, another mirror?
Because I am away from the country
where only the old and the impoverished cattle
share my pain?
My people's eyes telling my sister
she was a ten-rupee whore, a failed mother?
Perhaps the knowledge of seeing myself as I really am
would be a privilege, now that I am here.
In the peacock's blue and emerald feathered brocade
are the pulsing eyes of thousands of discontented workers.
In the luminous look of the cowherd god idol
lurks the dead gaze of Gandhi.
Hidden in the shadows of ruined temples lifelong
I waited for the last hour of my servitude.
To build a scene from secret harmonies,
not write a history of attitudes.
But all I have learned is to play my memories
on the instrument of my life,
as I sit with Hiromi or Hisami or Masako
startled with mysteries that seemed to wait
on a world beyond my own.
Like this, for instance,
so simple in Japan, without a need to understand,
the fact that when I told the truth in my land
it always hurt my mother more than pretending did.
Pain that we have learnt to take care of,
but not the deceit, bare and sunburned,
measure of the spilled blood of the wounded sun.

# Defeat

As a child, on my way to school,
I watched the fire crackle in the blacksmith's shop.
A boy sat, smiling, fanning the flames.
I didn't notice his eyes then, misty with pain,
or his hands as he worked with the bellows,
a finger broken, sores on his thin wrists.
A kingfisher swooped above my head, calling.
The morning wandered about at random,
neither real nor fiction,
the ruins of my grandmother's tales
where my voice trembled at the edge of things.
The blacksmith's shop is gone now,
and childhood sits in shadow
like an eye in a face that is dead.
So the door was opened to hunger and suffering.
Outside, the thick and strange movement
of human life. Today my old, insufferable mother
does not smile. She can't stop anyone
from a single suffering and so she can't stand
distance and silence. I look through
the morning into another distance,
where a dead turtle lies on the soft sand
of a beach. And into one morning, in which
miracles don't happen. Just the desperation
of standing at some invisible boundary
without being able to get past it.

# Nakedness

Yes, Runu,
it's you and I who are naked.
The winds rise kiteless,
and meat measures the speed of hooves,
as we let our sympathies
edge past the corners of our nakedness.

Here the dead always rise,
out of their eyes
appear the mist and the anguished pine.
So one among us begins a story:
yet how could one hear a voice
from the desolate stage?

Under the black stone
is another tomorrow:
a strange god who darkens
the pink hooves as you watch;
the design of the dead
you cultivate like a rose in a pot.

A way of telling each other
we know:
a curse of the rainbow,
my hands, lying open
one on top of the other,
cold as fish' on the slab of your lap.

# Possessions

Another day of waiting out, wondering
about our poets and what they are
going to say about us. In pain perhaps
they stand inside, but cannot
yet slam the door of their voice.
Still we do not think that God is cruel.
In the street outside, in naked poor twilight,
and a little tired, the minister
who finally had to resign;
his pride sitting quietly
in his chair, the bodies of five-year plans
strewn around, their mouths open to the sky.
The elections over, villages filling with shadows.
My father took four long years to die,
lying on the edge of his pus-filled bedsores.
My mother looked at him and took her pills
and pretended illness: it was only
the justification of her own life.
Death is never that simple.
Both knew that they were lying;
they did not turn their eyes away.
Maybe we all realize this, my friend:
that the life you allow me is your life.
Tonight, the politician will turn
on the country with his power.
His face will be well under control.
And tomorrow, sixty thousand children
will go hungry again.
Poets will sip their tea in stupid-looking cafes,
or dangle in unknown fields

like embarrassed scarecrows.
My neighbor's little daughter says
she can't understand why
the wind keeps crying in the telephone wires;
and there, how it makes the stars tremble too!
One doesn't know what to answer.
These days one can trust not even the light.
Over the fields beyond, the darkness seems alive.
Time, our strongest possession, bleeds.
It tastes salt and sickly on the tongue.
And always the waiting; a hundred years hence
the poems that torment us today
will still be luxuries;
hiding their impotent hatred
for the world's unresurrectable life.
Here I am tempted by freedom, affection, devotion,
the longing for nearness, the smell
of my lover's armpits, the round sensual contours
of women's bodies on the medieval temple
of Rajarani. Outside, by the unmoving wall,
a drongo begins to sing, sharply, insistently.
I wish someone could tell my son
that when I died, I died bravely.
But no, there is no real reason
for that either.
There is always a door open somewhere.
The trees never move,
yet seasons reason through their branches.
The worn-out face of India
has the weak eyes of poets
who die alone,
silenced by the shapelessness of life alive.

# The Captive Air of Chandipur

Every day, the ancient sea at Chandipur
spits out the gauze wings of shells along the beach
and rumples the air behind the burnt sands.
Who can tell us of the songs of this sea
that continue to bewilder us and double the space
around our lives? Or of the smells
paralyzed through the centuries, of deltas hard and white
that stretched once to ensnare the feet of women
bidding their men good-bye? Or of salt and light
that dark and insolent eyes demanded, their shoulders
languishing like lotuses in the noonday sun?
But what is it now that ravages the tide
in the shadow of this noble watercourse? The disdain
of the dead? Archaic sails still whisper
of tales on the horizon: who are you,
occupant of the silent kingdom of the conch?
The place looks empty now; and as we wait
for the tide to flood the mud flats
the song that reaches our ears is only our own,
the cries of fishermen come drifting through the spray
into the music of what the world has slowly lost.

■

# Traveler

Every evening
the bells of the temple close by
rest their easy weight on the bones;
it's time again to wonder
what I'll do with what I learn.
A warm vapor rises
from the darkening earth like a hope.
Somewhere, inside a room,
a girl is dying in her mother's arms.
Elsewhere, someone
revenges himself for his broken life.
I look at people. At my little misery.
Beyond, at a jasmine's sad, sweet smile.
Movement here has purpose:
It is not cold and tired.
The deer chasing the new growth of grass.
The drum thumping against the sky.
The woman with her knees drawn to her chest.
And the wind that deceives itself
it has tellingly carried the scream of the girl
who is dying in her mother's arms.
My knowledge and my time
fail to quiet to night
unlike the flutter of birds.
I try to wear this weight lightly.
But the weight of the unknown buries me.

# When You Need to Play Act and other Poems

Motionless. Still. Erect. Always
its truth, its rigid forbidding mood.
No time to look out and rejoice
in what one sees in it. Once, I remember,
as the flaming feathers of a dawn
bobbed through stubborn suns into a far skyline,
I thought maybe I might reach it,
but the skyline did not last long.
Sudden darkness burned it out: the awful spirit
that ruled our bones burnt our sacred gods,
turned our fathers' names to ash.
The sod hut of truth stood its ground,
where last summer fields of mustard floated
in the haze. Now what I see
might be half right, and like my room
this truth seems alive with its branded moves.
Has it told the old widow with the epileptic fit
to shuffle down the crowded road, showing
her blackened teeth, to lead me to my room, blind?
And the passersby to throng the diseased girl
who sits still and unmoving in the marketplace,
one full breast peering through
her ragged blouse, while her kindhearted parents

on whom she had turned her back
found it easier for them to meet their death?
No, never like the gentle breeze of a summer's night;
never never soft and loving
in your eyes as I follow the sunset
till all color drains from sky does it come,
to blind real nature and force
an adverse fate, a fruit, ready to the hand.
All truth is rather like a war.
Making love I chance to get a glimpse
of myself in the mirror, and I
long for another look. Because I cannot
grow a rose, I plant the seeds of the thistle.
So that we could crowd our battles down,
as one swats an injured fly. And I could say:
How can I be ready for life inside?
How could I have become engrossed
in something less crucial to see
finally my whole life pass before me?
How could the shadow
of hidden bones cast by the sun
drive out the iron from my wide open dawns?

# More in Dreams than in the Flesh

No wind. No storm.
Just the trees heaving in their own sorrow.
The girl next door who went missing a week ago
has come back; the faces of her parents stare
like bare, wounded hills beyond the river.
Often a dream makes one afraid
of the things one might do. It frightens one
that despair seems to have no boundaries.
The laments for a death are over while death
is warm and safe and drifts into sleep
in a child's dream.

Some time back I had stumbled
on the decomposing bodies of a young couple
on the hill slope behind the temple. The girl
couldn't have been more than sixteen years old.
I had made a great effort to defend myself.
Her half-open eyes now wander through
my subdued Sunday mornings as though testing
the courage it took to be a man.

No wind. No storm.
Just the vague light of daybreak
Coming down from the hilltops.
An unknown darkening is in my breath.
And I knew death is born to us in the same way
and when we cast our nets into the night
and draw in the shapes of day.

# Silence

Rain, all night.
Capacious, like the body of a woman,
And the heat, intolerable.
A cow lows once.

Strong smells of fish and palm-toddy in the air,
One doesn't wish to say anything at all.
How will one cross over?
The water, running out from the feet, ends up nowhere
The mountain's entire weight rests on the earth's body.

The saints are all silent inside their own truths.
Moss broods silently in the cracks of the stone.
Four-year-old Pratick is silent inside his screams.
Nobody answers him although they surround his fears.

And this evening, too, silent as yesterday,
swaying on its darkness inside the arithmetic of rain.
Into the moist eyes
of the young woman clerk, returning home,
a herd of shadows has entered
but somehow isn't able to come out.

How shall the evening star
give forth its light through the clouds?
Somewhere a garden spider
is busy, silently spinning its web.
Your sigh, too, has curled itself up
and lies asleep on a mat in the darkened room.

# Village Mythology

Flickering lamplight, fanfare of trapped wings,
Bears and snakes darken into another Orissa night.
The sea might sweep up on the shore again
in a sudden aggressive embrace. And walls
of madness rise up to the skies in a malevolent dark.
Yet one's earth is never in real danger.

Firewood on their heads, a file of women
stagger along the last rain-wet road.
Suna, the faithful village wife, crawls through darkness
as she moves beyond birth and death
from one night of rape to another.

Her destiny goes nowhere, but is everywhere.
The real story she listens to from her children
is made up of school, books and their bloodless pulp;
imagined loss somehow secretly feeds her sense of herself.
The anchor flounders in a sea without water.
In this forgotten sea, she is of the race
that can only sing of gods
who betray life with small embraces.

■

# A Hint of Grief

The rain is home, clinging
pitifully to the Orissa countryside.
Orioles rum on their wings of gold
where the sky falls into darker cloud.
Beyond the wood fence grow lotuses
and wild hyacinths of the wetness.
Again, from somewhere,
one calls back the love
of what one hungers to be touched by,
so I can call you by your name-Orissa,
as the wind returns again
for those empty voices it nurtures
in the thick-leafed mangoes and cashews,
and rain's frightened hands
drop the comic book of our history
onto the weathered stones.

■

# Bazaar Scene

"Where did you get the mango?" the mother
asked the excited three-year-old, taking
the soft fruit into her palm, knowing
exactly where it came from, eyeing
the rotting pulp already staining her fingers.
It was a time of jubilation for the chariot festival.
Indifferently I watched
the little pig-tailed girl running
down the road with a solitary mango
she had stolen from the vendor's basket, and
given to her crippled brother slumped on the roadside
The child looked so under nourished
his large eyes seemed ready to weep.
The golden weight of the piles of mangoes
on sale in the marketplace
points to that voice in us everyone knows,
a land of fluctuating shadow and sunlight
trapped in the roots of that mango tree,
a voice that is silent, fighting the poverty of fate.
A light rain suddenly wets the monsoon air.
A quiet movement seems to follow the running feet
of the girl whose silence keeps growing inside her.
And a mother's hand floats like a raft
endlessly down the river, still to find an end.

If the world weeps, are you moved?
Will it show you where to go?
Does the world grow according to its own needs?
Pity is only felt for one
whose eyes are blind to the ways of another.
With those eyes I cannot walk barefoot here.

# Living in Orissa

Something here, perhaps fatal spirit.
Something that recalls the centuries of defeat.
To live here,
antlered in sickness and disease,
in the past of uncomprehended totems
and the spilt blood of ancestors
one would wear like an amulet.
Today the darkness of our own shadows
slips over the uncared-for cemeteries
by the river.
Someone keeps walking down still
across the ravenous dust
between the graves,
waiting like an ancient debt.
And someone goes on dancing
at the doors of indifferent temples
carrying pain in an eyeless face.
Only shadows shift now.
They have the eyes of defeated spirits.
The old old eyes.

# The Woman Who Wanted to be Loved

Somewhere, a woman's body knows.
Rain is her mother,
a fitful time of sweat and tears.
Quietly she dies of ghosts of love
she found among the water and grass.

Her dark days cannot be braided into a poem.
But her body wants to escape from greater things.
There was a time when her breath rose up,
a flag to flutter in the wind. It was the hour
when her black hair with its long spears
needed the sacrament of blood.

Seasons pass, and she becomes stone.
Sighs of mango blossoms bring in
the scents of summer, scentless around the bone.
Love can break and still keep its promise.
It can borrow a dawn and haunt it through time.

# The Quest

Under the rain, beyond the walls,
I search for the lost inhabitants of my country.
Gleaming skulls of people I do not know,
those who had died a violent death
at the hands of a God with noiseless thunderstorms.
It has become a ritual, this search
for history in which dignity neither comes nor goes.
I wonder why they continue to suffer, and why
this private unhappiness of mine
demands a certain quality in the people I like.
The sadness of crows flutters down into the light.
The rain comes nearer. A tiger of jaws.
Yearly floods turn into a genuine poetic achievement.
Weary steel plants keep on going through the night
Even computers begin to understand our castes and prejudices.
The voluptuous figures of women in stone
only wish to save our feelings of love and freedom;
they are like old men who do not need their voices,
they have pulled them out of their throats
and hidden them away in their past.
I look into your eyes, trying to think
of newspaper headlines raising their hands
in a gesture expressing their inability to help.
The vicious assault on another young girl
progresses handsomely, breathlessly, without hope.
God still looks at me, his silence deep and famous,
the gaze of modesty touching earth and sky.
Searching for things in this land of rain,
I have really no intention of meeting inhabitants here.
And God? Do I have the need to create
another self whose laughter smothers my fears tomorrow?

# Sky without Sky
## Poems, 2018

### I

This is the Indian in me

Where does it all begin?
When the dying sun bleeds
The galvanized-iron sky orange,
When a dark absence leads one away
To the side of time where the dead walk,
And where the one leftover eye
Lies awake in the long night

When hope becomes a bird of prey,
Motionless, hanging above the good earth
As if it were its sole guardian.
When we don't like ourselves.
When there is so little physical unlikeness
Between one thing and another

And when first step towards
The time of rest becomes the longest walk,
The endless landscape of thought
Breathes a kind of music

II

Perhaps I am trying to think
of an aspirin pill
about to dissolve in a glass of water
or a monotonous metallic voice
dispersing in a deserted platform at nigh

So nothing else would exist

But a life, any life, If it is lived:
a map of a country one has never visited
and to find one's way in
one needs only know how to read the map

The snapping of the consciousness
to find a freedom
which could exist in a body
without parts of ourselves

And if I hear a sound like music
unlike any music I had heard

was it an answer
all the arguments in the world
can do very little about,
like a flurry of crows that rise
from a stubble-field and settle
on the boughs of unconsciousness?

III
Whether any answer attracts or not
it is within one
that it is born

A kind of music

Nothing that one can hear
in the silence everywhere
and then more silence

Reaching forward to that silence
I live
for that moment
when all thought
could achieve a vital synthesis

IV
Thought is a world made by you,
taught by you;
for a long time I know, since I was a child,
because you came to me
long before I knew how to listen to you,
and I could see you
long before I knew how to see.
You were already there,
survivor in the wildness,
catching up with the vast emptiness
of your shadow,
coming out of unmeasured time night and day
in the guise of a tree of bitter wood
to teach me theory, the melancholy of geometry,
and the possibility to live in a closed world.

V

Thought, when it's not made of words
an eye, breaking through in total darkness
prisoner in a cage filled with cranes:

When it comes, in a silence our voices
are unable to dissipate or arouse,
I am a startled deer which flees
Into the black syntax of weariness.

Perhaps this thought about words
is when it can't even pick a word,
the ambiguity of the play's final scene
when it's not clear if thought has fallen away;
or the darkness within that's falling,
unable to see where it was headed,
for everything everywhere
begins and ends in darkness.

VI

Even though nature was your world,
It was time to bring you down to earth.
Beneath that past was another past,
biding its time in the guise of a sun
that did not give off any heat or light.
Perhaps all that time you were scooping
pain and sorrow out of the body of the earth,
while around you was suffering, unseen,
suffering in the branches, suffering in the roots.
Like us, did you feel you were going into death
through fear of death?
Thinking to escape it as we go to meet it?

In fear of suffering, I come to you,
because here is death, and nothing to see.
You've moved away from your past,
lonely in your death, to show us
how necessary it is for us too, to die alone,
Each one, everything, every being,
all alone before nothingness, today, tomorrow.

Little were you aware then, you'd walk
this earth, always being where you were,
around of your heart, treading
so much space for so little matter;
with nowhere to go
but into yourself, where no other heaven
I mirrored, only the desire to feel
the happiness of being loved in the grand roar
of a world that lives on
with its senseless courage and its lonely misery;

with each new day you return
to noise and its silence
without seeking
an answer to it; an answer to yourself, as it were,
lost perhaps in the speechlessness of a magical forest,
that has no more scent, no longing, no dew,
or maybe it's in the wind that still sings
in the trees or in the shadows of the sorrow
that broke your youth when you needed it most.

Were you taking on the solitude of man
with an inner solitude,
more with the heart of air and water and sun
than under the rules of our eyeless world,

as we try to erase the threat of death
that stops us from doing what we want to,
holding our hands as though
we did not know what to do with them.

Where I am, my mind lost,
I let myself into this journey, darker than night,
where the crash of the sea
whispers under the blood roaring in my ears,
where I am caught by the nakedness of my life,
thrashing into your sleep
that moves neither forwards nor backwards.
And I observe nothing, with nothing I wish
to see, nothing I wish to understand,
because you cease to have any meaning:
just the poise of time deceiving myself into feeling
I was a puffball on a breeze
floating toward the beginning of the beginning.


VII
This thought:
is it really what brings me here?
The stillness of sighing driftwood
My sickening ancestry
Or dream that lives in fear of the world?

It buys tears for my eyes from nowhere,
longs for the lost scent of the rain
that never comes,
it walks alone along the streets of my death,
it keeps waiting to give birth to me,
having lost its mind for words.

Now when I think of myself,
I find how thought too
is capable of playing many selves,
that want to go beyond the destiny
that can't be addressed, never making their way
into the grammar of question and answer
because their uneasiness would reveal too much,

VIII
It could be your motionless body
the bare untouchability
the invisible wings you bear,
which give birth to thought.

It could be you plucked my mind
from its defiant stem,
conspired to make my weightless days
heavier than lead.

Now it's thought
that sits cross-legged on the floor,
as a contradiction of rage and pleasure
draws me into merciful darkness

for it to touch me again
and make me forget all thought.

IX

Our own world only goes where our eyes go,
and our own eyes make it,
turning time into thought,
whether it is the elegiac raindrop
that empties the world it falls into,
or the tide that bows courteously before death
each time it reaches the shore.

There's nobody but it
in the deep silence of the forest of your body,
silence a little deeper
each time there is no answer from you.

If your driftwood soul (in our eyes)
could swell up to the size of a neem tree,
there will no longer be
any difference between men.

X

To wait.
Until it comes.
This faith, that is your affair,
not ours.

No toy of a sentimental god
to play with.
No "Manifesto of Racial Scientists
to outlaw you.

Unlike you,
we are mere dreamers
who carry our consciousness
that only serves to show us
the nothingness that awaits us.

XI
Once in a while I blind my eyes
and climb the twenty-two steps
that lead toward unconsciousness

Once in a while I'd like to feel
the silence of the great earth outside
hoping to hear the faint cry of the soul

I've travelled a long way through the stars
trying your long silence
dying to be seen although I know I won't be

Only it's my dead grandfather I see
with his eyes of strange fish
Swimming in unknown depths

Perhaps a sleep falling over earth ad a
led him on, tying to its fragile thread
two things beyond belief: life and death

XII
Wisps of smoke
stand steep, then idle
over the *Swargadwara*.
Warm winds roil
the waters of the Bay
the sands quail.
I am one of them
who looks at the morning sky
and gets a sigh for an answer.

You do nothing: it is done for you.
What is beyond your gaze,
I will not know.
Because you will never be able
to do anything but accept,
always leaning against us,
bringing me back to where I ought to be.

We've believed in all of these.
But the morning is still unknown to me.

XIII
The house is full of eyes
some of elephants, some of mice

In the half-light
through the drawn darknesses of doubt

He sits on his throne
relaxed, hooded, extraordinary
Is he playing a game
that tests his knowledge, his wisdom?

Will he keep on urging me
to remember where I live, which my home

All those eyes
only crowd him out of the house

Do we recognize
the loneliness we think he deserves?


XIV
Who dances here?

Is it solitude
that puts its feet
in step to the plucked strings of loneliness
that guard your kingdom?


XV
In the core of your consciousness,
branches weep.

Mock sky of the earth,
your historic memory
more human than human,
loosens this intolerable loneliness.

Out of reaching hands,
when I step into your eyes,
just the parting of trees
where the river of unmeasured reason runs.

XVI
Through the little slow pastoral
by the tattered paddy fields
the still voice of thought
I thought
only my grandmother
                    knew,

skimmed past
the twenty-two steps
that led into the slow way
                    home.

I tried to step out of its path,
from the terrified iron wings
belonging to a hundred thousand shoulders.
I could tell nothing by its passing

I heard just the flutter of angelic birds
in the tree
that still stood in the depth of my heart.


XVII
Here is the thought we've bound and gagged,
that stopped to grow,
its voice of a victim, of stern, strangled thunder.
I build my steps on hollow hope,
dismissing the farewells
that stand on the roads by every milestone.
This heart is strangely silent,
having lost its voice
in the harem of veiled pleas;

and Sunday, the hidden talisman
which approaches from higher up along the road,
doesn't have the strength to live its hour,
to pick out the meaning of the shadows
that like to hide their little dirty hands
in the sulky, shriveled pages
of our mortally hurt lives.

They say life has a thousand or more doors
but it's hard to believe in the door
I'd enter.
The doors change shape and muscle

to become the voices
that beat strange and frightening wings as I wait,
to become a science
that's bloodless and uncomforting
into prayer that never gives even the doves
voice to my flight, soul to my loneliness.
It's hard not to feel the sympathy

of knowing one isn't alone
when I stand
on the planks of the worn wooden bridge of fear
across the slime-sunk heart
uneasy I can't make my steps a little longer.
It was the burning hunger
that waited on the sweaty steps at my door,
that made me gather my body
struggling under my feet,
that led me to seek an answer
in the uncertain, wishful breeze
rolling about in the high grasses of life.

Beyond,
children keep shouting in the comfortless city,

the wail of a cat rises, lustful,
to the moon,
men curse as they gamble with cards,
and a police siren chases
the wide Temple street away from its tame sorrow;
and in secret I see the transparent tints of the sky
float down fields and coasts,
scarred roofs and evening dusts,
into the immense solitude a child can only live in,
like, perhaps, the immensity of your sleep,
too vast and too old
to remember the real purpose of birth and death.

And I look into a world we'd known
that silently moves its face,
this god who had been plucked out of his home,
the slope of the mountain that swung in the void,
the drop of sweat that vacantly looks on
into the death that brought it to life.
There are those who call to us
to ask where we are.
How does one answer

when one can't keep thinking
about the course life had taken us along
the unfathomable distance
between my roots and my destiny?
Or, when I cling wordless
to my own punishments I create
to keep consciousness away from what I know is real?

XVIII

A winter sweep of migrating geese
is crying hoarse again in the high skies,
it's another unending day when it's hard to say
if the actor in the street-play is angry or amused,
like the priest who keeps frowning in the shadows
beyond the walls of monotonous funeral ceremonies.

A wind leaps across, released from the seas,
words of hidden crimes stifle the mind,
of abduction, rape and killings;
the bold injustices;
and I could hear the snarl of the beast in my voice
in the power I acquire
as I try to establish the wholeness of things
for no reason.

The thought that can't figure out what it wants
is a flower's that holds it
from merely becoming an aroma,
like a spider's academic wait which says
you're there to allow everything in the world;

the fervent prayer of a starving mother
stretched out around her only child
she has to sell to keep herself alive:
angels of thought
nestling in the old magic of dust,
the voice of memories of mystery

and of appropriate punishments for sins,
the uncertain intelligence of mine
which looks out of the narrow window of my prison cell

at a pale strip of sky,
thought that seduces others forgetting itself.

Among the longings for our lives
we cruise,
wordless in those histories, one for each one of us,
inventing ways to emphasize bitterness,
while thought is nowhere there
or becomes so heavy it can't be caught at all.
But at the oddest moments,
in the chaos of tears turning upon their pain,
there will always be a place to fill
and to dream of further places joined to that place,

this thing that made each one believe,
without knowing why
that this tree's last whisper was a silent one -
a silence that had sound, words, colours,
that make it move, then make it stop moving.

And I suppose this is all
about the moaning of faith
on the burden it carries:
the sunbird's need to plunge its head
into a deep-throated flower
and emerge in a flame of gold,
our journeys that deny the passage of time,
the garden where my fathers and fathers' fathers
who'd never let the long gleams of light
they had caught in darkness
slip out of their hands

as when
the wind comes on its own to the tree.


XIX
Even in Puri
when the world,
silent again
for a moment,
begins to speak again,
I long for Puri.


XX
It's more or less
as though you cut a deal.
When one mask dies on you,
you are ready for another one.
Maybe, in exchange,
you live the full life
you've always wished for.
It's the face of the mask
that has caught you
on the sanctum sanctorum
of your nerveless gaze.

How easily one misses
the masks response,
as it savors its triumph!
How it moves gracefully
as a ship under sail,
when the wind behind it
goes into light around you!
No outside force

orders your life. Or, does it?
In time,
greedy grasping hands
turned yours into wings,
yet the wings never caught the wind;
the smoke from a million fires

rises and dies
through the sockets of your skull.

Now, in another forest,
abandoned to the inexpressible,
you watch
light blind memory,
as you look out
from a house of light
with the smile of someone
planning to feed the birds.

It's the way, they say.
What sort of road are you?
Where do you lead?
No stale masks of countless years

can mute the howl
of the coiled serpent
which has no form but lives
in all things.
Your masks have no dreams,
removed far from things
not to be seen, heard,
or known about,

And forgotten
in the play of our desires,
8ven away
to our small understandings,
you go on carrying all Odisha
through the boundaries of your gaze,

leaving me a solitude
where I have no right
to my death, or to the lives
I've lived before;
here, I'll sit on the steps
of my door, and I'll sleep,
coming up to myself, meeting myself.



XXI
In a darkness we've made for you,
this dark that never asks or wonders,
you've made us live our lives,

Are we lost, living
in the way we have?
Have we loved
living in the dark you mirrored in us?

I can't put it out of my mind
that I've more than a thousand faces.
The first I lost eighty years ago
when our family visited the Temple
and a piece of your darkness
splashed like a raindrop on my human race.

The light from the oil lamps
bowed in a purpose I didn't understand.
A world stood still in the room.
Abandoned to darkness, to fog.
to the pitiless silence
and to windowless, doorless obscurity.

And then, those eyes;
an end like all other ends in life,
wordless, overwhelming
It's there, the door;
and I am standing outside
but will not yet risk the first step.

For if I take it, I know I'll lose myself.
But I'm already on my way.

I am already on my way.
My face pressed into a function
in that giant, vital graveyard
where the dead dream away their death
but cannot enjoy it still.
And those eyes
frozen in their nakedness,
in their inescapable humanity.

A thousand years older now,
I feel something open within me
and pour like light
into the narrow space

between sleep and wakefulness,
something unknown

like a tenderness sculpted by the fingers
of the wind.

And I felt my breath move softly
and my life move, like my breath,
softly,
into you, out of you.

XXII
History blossoms in your eyes.
No matter how you came to be,
no matter if our selfishness
helps make your stark beauty,
no matter it comic demons like us
drive you to act as though
you were a normal human being
you are memory, pushed by purpose
into our weary existences.

From your inconsequential throne,
mass graves in your eyes
wander the whole yawning world
that holds us in thrall
as it disappears like a chirp in the air
when the bird is gone.
Thought is what's left behind
the sacred, immutable chant
of ceremonial gesture.

XXIII

This thought, this faith I never have,
is neither clear like spring water
nor muddy like a limping sewer,
I feel its lily-white arms embrace me
but end up nowhere.
In a bond that could never be ours
it comes to be born, to make me
sleep it away for the rest of my years.

Most of the time
the little handful of peace it promises
is like a street-play: if it's a success,
it must find the courage to lie.
To hunger, to iron, and showy storms
of obsequiousness and pitiful betrayals;
we've made it sit on a throne, an oppressed emperor
it never has, in invisible robes,
embraced us with its lily-white arms,
looking around to see if only
it has squandered away the precious times.

XXIV

And inside the thought they must have said
to themselves: Why is a deformity like him
worshipped as the "Lord of the Universe?"

I take my own measurements
of the exaggerated austerities of my patience
that challenged me with words
which only left me alone.

I watch the twilight in the look in my eyes
and say:
> That's the beast.
>  That's the mouth on the mouth.
>  And that the only hunger under the sun,
>  wild as the tides of the Puri Bay
>  with no heart of escape,
and it understands nothing.

Now nothing moves in my hands.
And shadows are shadows
waiting to be freed and die.


XXV
Because you're there.
Because you make me forget
the wasteland encircling us
and which I still cannot.

After all that's been said,
all that's been done,
all that has been thought, dreamt,
fashioned, built, chanted
so much faith spent
and then faith can be no more.

And because I can still hear
the faint flutter of birds
in the tree
that stood in the depth of my heart.

XXVI
the
slow falling back
from
a field
of fulfllings

# Poems from "Relationship"

### One

Once again one must sit back and bury the face
in this earth of the forbidding myth,
the phallus of the enormous stone,
when the lengthened shadow of a restless vulture
caresses the strong and silent deodars in the valley,
and when the time of the butterfly
moves inside the fierce body of the forest bear,
and feel the tensed muscle of rock
yield to the virtuous water of the hidden springs
of the Mahanadi,
the mystery of secret rights that make up destiny:
and to clasp the slow slopes of stone again
that ascend to the realm of the dead,
slopes that stroke the mind
with their quiet faces of sorrow,
like that of old men curling for warmth
in the winter sun,
and of young ochre-clad prophets
laden with silent fulfilment of tomorrow.

We have come as dreams disguised that pinned us down,
artisans of stone,
messengers of the spirit,

twelve hundred artless brown flowers in passion
to the night in humble brotherhood,
aerial roots of a centuries-old banyan tree;
not taking lives seriously
for our lives are only of the seeds of dreams,
forgetting the cruelties


of ruthless emperors who carved peaceful edicts
on blood-red rock,
forgetting our groans and cries,
the smells of gun smoke and smouldering flesh,
forgetting the tactics and the strategy
that led to the founding of the infinite distance
inside our watery skulls.

Time
and the boat,
the initiation into the mystery of peace;
the sailing ships of those maritime ancestors
who have vanished in the black Bay without a trace,
that only live in the sound of the waves
flinging themselves on to the dark fringes
of this land from Chilika to Chandipur.
But time has no mouth,
and the black labyrinth
of casuarinas along the edges of the sea
closes the sky's eternal vault,
tall and brutal,
trapping the evenings' first stars of haunting order
and the solitary traveller
who can sense the brilliant colors of the past
in the ocean's strange and bitter deeps,

that subterranean river in the rock
which admits him with dignity
into some fresh wonder of its flowing.
Now caught in the currents of time
I watch the blue of the sky
seep out slowly,
hear the voices of old waves drift into silence;
and yet my existence lies in the stones
which carry my footsteps from one day into another,
down to the infinite distances, the dense jungles

where tigers eyes are glowing red.
like virulent boils of pox on dead women and children,
and where the grotesque dawn of wilderness wood
becomes a conceiver of life, nothing else,
as I continue walking back and forth
not knowing whether the earth
would let me find finally its mouth;

only that the stones were my very own,
waiting as mother or goddess or witch,
as my birth feeds on them
as though on the empty dugs of sorcerous thought.

**Two**
Today I watch through the window
the grave that is my mother's,
watch the old impulses in red and yellow
chalked across the white terraces of childhood,
in the shores of distant refrains,
as a member of some magician's audience
watches a white rabbit
flash out of the excited applause

and vanish in the air,
or as a fraudulent reflection
recoils from a warm summer afternoon,
just as a thin veil of light drops
the distant mountains through the open door
        of my flesh,
and the unidentifiable dead shadows
strip the skin off my face,
and from the body of the last green spring
memory takes a road vague with the distance
        of loneliness and hurt,
away from the terrible glance of sky and its forest
where cranes bound into the surrounding silence
of wounded pools of our living.

Orion crawls like a spider in the sky
while the swords of forgotten kings
rust slowly in the museums of our guilt,
while the carved rock loses its light,
and the man with many memories
doesn't know what to do with them,
with the river flowing sluggishly through his dark,
for the boats he let loose upon the water
merely bob up and down, going nowhere;
as the grass of history
merely glistens tor a moment with night dew, merely
that,
and my memories are just voices of another world,
pretending from the throat
where the distant music of stars cuts blood,
and the suffering of the world returns
like winter's persistent asthma
year after year.

Now like my quickly-aging father
my mind fumbles at the frail substance of ash,
and my memories are rats scampering in the dark
gnawing at rotting paper,
twisted metal and foul flesh,
and my blood becomes to share his curse;

as I forget easily
my old village's pelt, glistening with rain,
and the stillness of my gentle daughter's skin,
forget the desire
oozing out of the hewn stones of Konark
and the voices of frogs
bending the white-wet moonlight into embraces
through the strange fires that carried him down
from the tranquil hills in the rain.


**Three**
Here is the tapestry of the year's first rain;
like an army, uniformed in gray,
but penitents, down on their knees.
What can ever wash the air of its gashed voices?
It is hard to tell now
what opened the anxious skies,
how the age-old proud stones
lost their strength and fell,
and how the waters of the Daya
stank with the bodies of my ancestors;
my eyes close now
because of the fear that moves my skin:
the invaders walk along the only road they know
that leads to their bloody victories.

Ah Father!
You recognize the sounds
of your children's laughter before it comes,
and the whispers of gods
before they crumple under your children's feet.

These nights of the growing moon
fill us with the feeling of good;
that is exactly what you wished for us,
didn't you, Father?
So our courage would be swept away
by the fierce winds of summer dust?
So we would go on
reading the epics in the lamplight,
sucking our mother's dry and drooping breasts,
watch the thin moon blend into that darkness
where gigolos and pimps and bums
jabber excitedly in a language of monstrous flowers.

I remember only last week I counted up my friends,
and I felt as though I were in painful exile:
friendship is like a pool of water
where shadows move about and dance,
and winds of doubt cloud some of the drifting faces,
the sun of envy sucks the others away.

Dust and the sun tear open our timorous voices.
What is it I want to hear
when I look into the eyes of the hunter
as an iron mist takes possession of me again,
as the words of mine that yearn for rain
catch only the jagged lightning of this new cult
          and its messianic gain?

Out of the darkness, the ash:
I won't touch it, my fingers let the grains slip by,
my hands are weak for the violent life,
the window looking out onto my mother's grave
        defends my dream,
one which I have never understood through the years,
as though it were a sky full of fallen birds,
as from its depths
a cloud drops its rain
onto the great silence over the stone of fire.

Now you don't even want me to write my poem,
of those words which spit blood and vomit and speak of
malice,
but only those which shut out the wind
and lay them in the dark crevices of stone
for births to merge into darker births
that look for the age-old grass of my death
beyond its contemplation and its withering.

Four
So the sleep you wear yourself to
through the smouldering burning-ground
        of your granite eyes
or through the birds alighting tamely
on the warm indigo waters of the tropics:
colourless and dreamless, a light without leaves,
will not reveal the truth of that secret miracle
of the darkness that hangs over the screams
of the hyenas or the snarls of the bears,
when, afraid of the silence that lurks inside
        the dawn of your startled smile,
the thousand windows of my sorrowful heart

look upon your untempered mile
that wanders through the eternal half-light of rain.

Is this
simply a craving to let myself go,
to bury a drug-drop of today's bitterness
in the pit of my heart?
My fear receives no one;
like a flame which sings on altars of the dead,
isn't it strong enough
to shed the blood from the veins?

Burden of your peace, Father

Theme-song of my life that bums my tongue

Voices of children always wronged


And now, you, my ancient love of a hundred name,
of rains and endless skies and morning mists,
of wind-beaten evenings or owl-calls and rice-harvests
            in December,
my love of gold nose-rings and laughing earrings,
of towering ruins of stone panting in the dark,
of loyal lions guarding the diamond navels of shrines,
of amber breasts and secret armpits,
of cries and the soft steel of thighs,
and of the old emptiness of my own destiny;

I know I can never come alive
if l refuse to consecrate at the altar of my origins
where the hollow horn blows every morning

and its suburban sound picks its way
through the tangled moonlight of your lazy sleep.

Here now is this aging, my chance and sentence,
calmly circling hawk-like overhead for prey,
as the earth glistens with old mountains
and moaning rivers that satisfy
the solitudes lingering in the open talk of men.

But lying upon my loneliness
this brassy October afternoon,
the secret coves on the naked beach
charred by old fires and littered with
picnic-paper and empty bottles,
I want to finish my prayer that began
like a thin rustling in a mango tree
a prayer to draw my body out of a thousand years
and reflect the earth's lost amplitudes,
the bridal footprints of fantastic peacocks dancing
        in the rain

and the warm palms of gathering dusk
where crimson heart-lines float longingly
in the unknown sunlight of the earth,
like soft cirrus crossing space above,
and my dark heart twists
with a feather of your unheard moan,
weary with an echo
of your goodbye of tasteless ash.

**Five**

So I shall seek the sleep-habit
of the golden deer, tempter of the tastes,
in order that I might see outlined
against the vast forest of the heart
the miracle of living, so that others may pity me,
so that my dream would not end:
the fabulous marriage procession of power, like Siva's,
and the different dimensions of lies and betrayals
in order to survive,
the strange country
in which you weave your flaming play.

This sleep was needed,
to go on pretending that blood throbs
in the pallor of dreams, to find
the enchanted regions of boyhood and dignity
where the burnt granite of the fallen Konark
binds the sun to a rhythm of desire,
and the supple figures multiply
their mute echoes of another fire on stone.

What other answers can one think of
on a late autumn night,
when centuries drift quietly in the air,
rising like a mist from the steaming rivers
towards this visionary part of one?

Thus the naked wall,
groping through wind and rain,
that speaks back without sound or voice
and yet anoints our eyes with blood,
to wreck frantic vengeance

with its earth of acid ground;
a sleep of swamp grass and mangroves,
like a humid fever,
which protects the shores of life from savage storms.

What sea leads your blazing rivers
headlong into it? Were you worked up
by the gold quarries in that twilight place
where the phantom darkness
glowed red like blood? Were you guided
by the premature deaths of those frightened virgins
who fought the light of the stars
in their underground caves only to fall
at the darts of fretting virtue
This sleep is a song
that is heard from all sides continually,
a Coarse cage that can hold a larger life,
a time that stretches the scarlet in the mind
and graces the heart's skies with clear wind,
the hiding-place without beginning or end,
and the largest circle that transcends
the angles of man's consciousness,
a blind eye that creates the special vision
of our poignant significance.


**Six**
And how shall room be made for sleep,
how shall the wind be made to carry
the lioness 's roar, the endless ritual
of the black kites on the faraway hill
silenced in the whiteness of the clouds?

Voices go in and out or the city gates;
the moment the storm blows, I know I will scramble
to hide the thunder in the thick jackfruit groves
on the other side of the wall,
blackening the seeds of the fruit,
and reddening the soft gums of the unassailable flesh.

I look through the swollen grass of noon
and in the heart of great gray clouds and cutting rains
the autumns of a thousand years
spread out like leaves, filthy and veined with blood,
over the smooth dark stone of our lives:
what can save us now
but the miracle we have been waiting for?

The clock,
stabbing in a cobras tongue across the air,
an unknown bird
brushing past with a flap of wings
like the unseen wind scalloping the silence
out there in the bleak cremation ground;
no, there is room enough for cries and whispers,
for a nameless sigh, for the sharp blade of love,
for another kindredship of spirit to spread over my face the
        magnesium of a smile,
for a new body to reveal
the green-leaved carpet of pleasure,


somewhere, elsewhere,
wearing the dreams away of the forgotten Ganga kings,
digging at the ruins of their own private sorrow.

## Seven

How long does it take one to know
that it is he who is standing there,
alone by himself in the witness-box
of shackled pink muscle?

Once again
the heavy round night rolls on my pillow,
the weight of shadows of sick relics lies upon the bed,
time to realize that martyrdom is not for those
left alone in that no-man's land
where venison tastes like cottonwool,
and where the seated Buddha of my urge and will and
pride
would topple from the poisonous bite and acid
of the subtle bird of night,
but to find again the five shadows
which would help avenge the cooled motionless blood,
the elephant of the six blind men,
the crude murders
and the haughty seasons over man's eyes,
the rules of our song
that can only move back and forth
like a galvanometer needle
Between the zero and the hundreds of gloom.

Therefore into the pit of feverish sinews
and spring seashells let me fall,
for only by conquering them
Can one conquer the rest of the world,
and the empty shore then
thunder with the red lightning of the hermit crabs,
and the sense of empty sadness

turn into the mangled skeleton
of a sleep.

And let the wild harmoniums play on,
the wooden soldiers marching not knowing where,
in my thick insomnia,
to the beat of drums
heralding the periodic invasions of the enemy
into the vanquished city
and I remember your trembling
through the deserted ashes of my heart
that will already have been sold,
and the dark worn steps are marked
by the green rain of centuries,
shadows of my blood waving their pretentious hands.

### Eight

It is my own life
that has cornered me beneath the stones
of this temple in ruins, in a blaze of sun.
Sun-lions, standing against the steps,
whose return to life are you waiting for:
Whose roar to pulse through the veins
of this first night of sleep?

Far into these granite peaks of dream
where the air is moist and soft in the smell of the sea,
where the dying child lays his father on the sands
blind solitude,
where there swills about us
the spacious body of woman, the fruit and the flower,
the gentle leaf, the folded belly
and the sweeping fire,

like the warm waters around fish,
like the velvet down about the floating breath
        of fledglings.

So through this door, through
the gleaming skin of the three kingdoms,
the mineral, vegetable and animal,
to experience the fever of love
and the deeper undulation of the earth.

        Would meaning remain
in merely that a thing exists, on a single plane,
in the helpless sips of loneliness we have made,
marooned on the stone, on the dark chariot of the sun
whose fevered granite wheels claw desperately
at the strangled earth in our lives?

These things, hewn out of the darkness
and of the light, of our ominous destinations,
of the real and the imagined:
the bronzed gazes of mermaids
against the infinite blue of the sea,
the night of wild elephants pounding down
        in the undying sun,
and the horned and the hooved,
the *gandharvas* and the demons,
aren't these mere imitations we have made
not having had enough of the suns flight
across the purple hills of our guilt,
and the haunting dawn whose convex arcs of light
correspond to the dark abyss
an absent dimension of the blood?

This is the real body: raging pachyderm
with the crazy testicles, red and wild,
the lusting god of the blackest Siva night:
thus it is that it can hardly contain ourselves.
For it is no use trying to keep it away,
the quinine of this silence, the cloud of my
would your unborn rain show me
the colours and contours
of the distant valleys of birth?

For now I touch your secret order,
embarrassed *yoni*;
before me lie the sulking years of dreams,
the stricken purposes of the muscles,
the violent splashes of sunsets
in the fibres of the being.

How would I pull you out
of the centuries of fallen stone?
How would I hold the *linga* in the eye
until the world is made all over again?

**Nine**
This must be the myth of every happiness,
the high wind that flings the flowers into disarray,
the adamant bones which keep rolling in the dust
        of the dark butterflies,
the cry of the wounded sun silenced among
        the ruins of Konark.
I thought: those who survive the myth
have slipped past their lives and cannot define
        their reason,
the trees are getting sparse, the clouds dwindle

                into colder air,
the ancestral fires are no more snares,
purposes that resembled the webs of the sun
are lost in the silences of corners of dim rooms
where only ideas, like brooms,
wait oddly on their unstable heads.
Once it was a season, it was a bride
I dragged in its joyous flower-pot into the middle
                of my life:
my dead grandfather floated in that sea of buried things,
wings ablaze with a silver fire,
as if his body of stone were a pyre
burning on in that razed city of the ambitious walls.

Those who've been my friends throughout the years
have known only how to keep walking toward
themselves,
along the upraised road, unsullied by guilt and belief:
the rapture of ownership on their voluble faces,
their satisfaction stained green
by the green of the mango trees of the delta,
the green of banana and the green wind in the tamarinds,
and strangely cold by their own mistrusted
                of the inextinguishable ash.

I tried to speak of the myth of sleep and action,
in the hope of soothing myself and those others,
rummaging through the secret blo0d
                of the wind in the pines
and awaiting the deepening nature of all things
a perfection I'd prove to myself,
The honesty that holds the throat of man
against the light and looks down at my hands

and scales the anguish passing from man to man
to reveal the coarse need
that still can make one love a neighbour;
and at the savage blooming of some common stone
that calls to me from its mystery and its dream,
and which resembles the unexplained feeling
        of a mother
when she gives her breast
to her dry neighbour's bawling child.


And I heard someone speak of it there below:
where the bamboos sag like sad-eyed widows in worship
into the stagnant village pools,
in which naked children sleep for ever
among the green coils of the water-lily,
and where a dark-eyed woman climbs the endless stairs
of her abandoned house, the great earth
cowering before her, turning back
the triumph of death with the power
of her faithful silence, outside the bonds of time,
and where the mysterious shadows lurk under the leaves,
dispersing the past over the bends of the Mahanadi.
But what was this myth? It was like a leaf
whose trembling held my hand;
the colossal temple had crumbled in the unknown past,
onto the sandy bank of a vanished river
which once had dominated the heart of the wind.
What was the myth, a journey in which one feared
one could lose oneself at any moment? Or was it
merely a time which lay in the dust and stone
of the languid water, which moved sadly
about the absent jasmines only to be heaped
against those unreachable shores?

It is no use now if I try to wear
my grandfather's smile, disappearing for an instant
in the midst of this myth; there are shadows
over my body, from the burning sun,
there are structures which flank the river,
lacquered in red and gold,
Sundays with savage afternoons
and shriveled steps dangling from the shrines,
mirrors whose images throw
involuted rainbows into faces,
there are prostitutes with white hair
who are excited simply by having stared
          at their inaccessible sons,
and friends whose eyes are black and bitter with malice
like envelopes with poisonous glue on their flaps
because they are positioned by an ignorance
          in my heart,
and newspapers that bend our minds
          with gleaming and immaculate words,
and daggers that are anxious to return
          to the naked flesh,
and the shameless fevers
          whose viruses tear the skin like paper.


**Ten**
So many times I have stumbled out of my door,
proud of that time I had held hidden in my hand,
to see the sage of troubled mien
sitting under the peepul tree, all alone,
unspoken repose against the body oozing of love;
and, going past, in the act as though
of repeating a mistake, walking slowly toward them

in the swathe of indifference snaking out of their eyes
to make me accept the silence of which I was in fear.

For it seemed to be a time
when waters flow past without their purposes,
when replicas of temples lie scattered everywhere
and thousands of fake huge eyes open wide in wood
        inside them,
and bees become the lost witnesses
        of an unknown honey before the storm.

And if it was the time, I thought,
to be conquered by a sleep that had come to rest
on the unmoving dreams of our past,
it would only help to free the darkness
        that lingered on the mossed walls of my life,
and on the twisted bones
        that plunged through my volcanic flesh.

For there, ahead in the growing distance
where the myth appeared to cut the instant
        in light and shade,
a giant tree speechless above the sacred hill,
scores of women waited, their heads
        covered with devotion,
like the leaves, shaking as though possessed
        with spirits malign;
and the town of Cuttack where I was born,
its lanes scarred by ruts from whose clay
the goddesses take their sacred shapes
in autumn every year,
and looking out into the endless Bay;
mysterious inheritance

in which roots stick out here and there from the dung
of broken empires and of vanquished dynasties,
and of *ahimsa's* whimpers;
for before I go to sleep
or go into the unknown in me:

this house of blind windows built inside,
doesn't the fear it provides accelerate
       our happiness?

We are delivered by the myth
which exhorts our sleep and our losses
that wakes us like toys springing out of a box,
opening out like humiliating episodes
or dutiful monuments that celebrate
the victories of that darkness over us

Perhaps it came out of a ruined birthplace,
from the last barren heath we could not cross,
to set feet on top or the massive stone;
that was to be the first hiding-place
and whose ruins would remain forever
to defy the progress of our race,
as we felt the black slime of lotus-root
move slowly through our bone,
copying the reeds in the river as they bend
       in the current,
to give way to the river-silence
of aging timber lining the morose banks.

Now I stand among these ruins,
waiting for the cry of a night-bird
       from the river's far side

to drift through my weariness
listening to the voices of my friends
who have become the friends of others,
Writing poems, abject and anxious,
in rooms which reek of old folk,
of their sloth and arthritis and neglect,
like stale cupboards which are going black
with the smells of the rancid fat of the past.

## Eleven
Yet what holds back my voice is only a mirror,
the sound of the answer from these pitted ruins,
through the hollow, unreal space of the stone
like the flesh hollowed out by the years in a woman,
fragrant of old sandalwood and the dawn light of fish
that opens a flight of steps behind,
down which the unfelt beat of the heart
becomes deaf to everything,
all else being taken up by a possession.
Then can the present be recognized, what one endures
and one will continue to endure, a kind of world
that comes up of all the love he has known,
so that man can see from the vast night around him
the beauty soar into the sky,
into the tangles of cloud and rain,
of that drowsy voice calling
from other people's lives.

For lofty as they are on their twenty-four blue spells,
my walk along the tremblings of the stone
seems loftier still; to the flashing tendril
from the fugitive root, the throat of stone
choked with the many truths of eternal sleepers,

gently over the precarious tiers
as I put my hand toward a dream the sun
has kept awake through the years.

And at last there
where the day sweeps its aggressive yellow curves
like a serpent-woman's tail,
is the space, defiant, waiting,
and the iron sea of years ago curling about the feet,
a phosphorescent glow, an essence divine,
small yet huge enough to fill
with the velvet storms of pink lotuses,
and with the desire of my hands
I draw day unto myself, trembling with being,
the sky and the vine that will become
the exile for night to hold,
trembling with each new moment to a gold,
each woman's breath of moist grass
and her thresholds of milk
to a red meat or grace.

**Twelve**
        Fear of my guilt, I bid you farewell.

When the waves come, following one another,
the silence and the noise,
the banished princess and the magnolia tree as well,
a song rises from the honeycomb latticework of stone
to grip these bones where
a gray water of blood stretches out to the future.

Is anything beyond me that I cannot catch up?

Tell me your names, dark daughters

Hold me to your spaces

In your dance is my elusive birth, my sleep
that swallows the green hills of the land
and the crows that quicken the sunlight in the veins,
and the stone that watches my sadness fly in and out
of my deaths, a spiritless soul of memory.

# Hesitant Light (2016)

## The Crossing

Cruel seem these bars, the sun so narrow,
I am my home, they say,
for once here, there can be no farewell,
this is my first tie
as my heart beats into barriers of night.

Here play the winds of the world,
the sky too in its uncanny distance.
I stand on an empty promontory
watching the invisible wave
that goes on beating against my will.

The journey too slow,
and already in the far distance.
But God's excuse is that he doesn't exist,
in the cry of the lonely island
as though it had never been.

The bars were always there, the other ones,
and the ones that were to come,
the bars of the playpen of childhood
or of the beliefs that rule our dawns
from day to day;

And now should I tie my life
that is being born out of death
for one night, realizing well
that the morning
already means farewell the living never ask?


The wind rushes on,
between the clumps of knowledge
and the wrought-iron gate. And I,
at the end of the world I feel is mine.
My breath hangs white in the air.

To wall the wind, to triumph and defeat,
respectful and quiet,
just watching how this body of mine
would like it to be used.


**Crossing the River**

Her face buried in their rage,
the stripped, naked Kondh woman
writing on the forest floor
can only implore
her deity of the silent trees

to pull down those leaves upon her.


What else could they want,
besides plotting her every shame,
and abetting
the weaknesses of their god?

Moments of snide laughter
rest in the hands of her tormentors
tor more torn tomorrows,
while golden blooms dance on her body:
mustard, turmeric, sunflower,
only in torture
those good-natured suns of her dreams.

And a slow scarlet sunset
climbs down
the dark foreheads of branches
and turns its face into darkness.
The first sleep is the blessed sleep.

Back in the city
the quivering night
has bent backward
over the railings of the public park,
losing its voice in pleasure and pain.
The pallid eyes of street lights
fill with tears from a swath of rain,
as nakedness leans
against the walls of moonlight elsewhere,
a faithless shadow
that mocks time

on the crime they'll commit again tomorrow,
and a white ceiling moves in the sky,
more than white, unhooking her eyes
with which the earth had held her earlier.

## Solitude

In the lonely part of Alice that stops
at the threshold, in the small girl's fear
that moves her lips and is unable to talk.
Because that is what it does, waiting for us,
feeds us with itself, drives us till we wear away.
I climb down childhood, and see nothing,
no one, no return, no lovely rose light
that leaps in the far depth of wonderland.
Just those faithful dogs eyes, and I can
do nothing unless it moves on.

It's not the slow drip
of the sky's immensity that concerns me,
the ridiculous panic on the razor's edge
that settles hold of me one instant
and is gone the next,

but the way I lay down my newspaper
on the bench, turn my wrist over and look
at the time by my watch. My own world
is so small. I'm always in front of myself.
I touch. And these walls,
the slightest of sunsets behind them.

## The Weight of Yesterday

Memory deserts me today.
A rose still blooms in silence.
I have no letters to burn.
I look at the cottony clouds,
fail to rise into the air.
Light does have to be made.
I cannot distinguish
the rainbow rising from the heart
of the waveless sea.
The rain bleeds
through each farewell that befalls us;
this is a land without light or color.
Memories have left no tracks.
Maybe this was to be expected,
for they beat, far beyond
the windows of my prisons
with their homesick, remorseless rhythms.
The country of frozen winds
stretches toward an unknown horizon.
I look into its rusty haze

which reflects only those things
that did not happen.
Nothing touches me now,
not even the wet night
burning into my skin.
The rain finds its way back
to the door that has been
always left open for it.
And I go on looking for mine,
as I pass by the unchanging garden

that speaks no bond and no farewell,
whose flowers press up a cry in me:
the unheard scream of all dead marionettes,
the roses who have pulled up
their legs fearfully into their bellies.

## Not to be Loved by a Poem

Words believed me, I'd always thought,
yet one more word from me
would fleck my face with blood.
The afternoon behind me, shuffled on,
Phlegmatic and docile, in my tracks.
And a delirium of emptiness
opaques the windows
through which I keep hurting myself.
Sitting back, staring at nothing
I'd like so much to believe in myself;
and yet, my mind could not accept anything
no place to come ashore,
just the right to run for my life.

In such a place
where each one plants situations
for the other to find, I groan under
the weight of some meaningless confusion
as I lie awake in my embrace,
blind as the one who pushed me there.
I think about love, cold predator,
who watches me through
the thicket of my memories
for any movement that had made me
thirstier than I had ever been.

Perhaps nothing I can say or do now
will repair things.
From the river the cold wind carries home
various scents: anecdotes of life,
the fear of betrayal by a poem,
or an evening crouched
over the uncertainties of the coming night.
Nothing's ever happened yet.
Just the afternoon,
standing at the graves of our fathers
or a poem, abandoned
with our weak, defenceless bit of heart:
a dead fish,
bruising the vast white belly of light.


## Rain

The scent of black soil.
Slush on the canal banks,
along the shacks
sluggishly pressed against each other.
Nobody talks about the world outside.

Beyond the darkness
the fiercely rising river
No stars shiver in it.
A glowworm, generous in its light,
flies me into darkness.

From some doorway
small notes of a song slip by.
It's a pulse beat,

bringing in a memory, a road
or lie for one to carry on,
or a something that allows me
to be part of who they are.

Bicycle bells slow down
the rain's drowsy fall
The cool night air seems real.
Somewhere, someone
is at a summer story once again,
with words that only work
in the real world, where
we live on without knowing.

## When the Shadows Would Leave

Here, I have no choice
Up close, the air is crisp,
caught in the breath of cinnamon
and grass.
I've given it a name: winter.
Perhaps time to leave the rain behind
to its restless peace. To pull me
right out of things, out of this world
with its long nights.
Perhaps it's all about the strength
to live, is this moment,
because I've lived this far
and am so engendered; because

I'm still alive, and death
succeeds in making us betray those we love
as we practice our inexcusable behavior.

And winter, as I realize
I'd have to end it
with its pages of random characters
yet again the cool inquisitive north wind:
that has made people believe in love,
the salt shallows of Lake Chilka that shrink
as flocks of flamingoes winter over,
and the one lonely house in the valley
finds a way to live off the stiffness
of absences and the river to0,
with its gaze of peace determined to reign.

Nothing is disturbed,
but even at the chirp of a sparrow,
I cup its twitter in my closed fist
as if I were holding a moment of death
tight inside itself.
I'd really like to measure the steps
I walk on, to believe that I don't want
anything of myself to remain, but that
would be a crude picture
of the remotest loneliness.

The winter fields lie on their backs
in a corner, hearing nothing, seeing nothing,
I wish I could put something between myself
and the world that could be a defence
against more than physical danger.
And you, a whiteness at the sky's edge,
unable to prevent something other than itself
from existing, this hour before daybreak
which is not yet day;
it is winter,

the huge electric turbines at the river's edge
go on turning by themselves,
a shaft of new light sings like wet grass,
green and heavy with smell,
and I can feel the whole weight
of the world's sinking, sleeping head
against my fingers.


## Blue of the Sky

Its hard hidden stone
overlooks the growing trade of blood

between brother and brother
who still go on talking of Truth

And of those who would appear to arrange
the world as best as they can

Old widowed violins of legends
fill the air with a mute sleepless wailing

It looks on the trees wearing the blood of men
for clothing instead of leaves

and on the hazy memories that are all
men can achieve at the end of their lives

It wonders at the earthworms of solitude
still gnawing the desperate bones of the dead

and follows the terrible look of cities

which keep a prisoner of the sun

And at the crude prayers that stand guard
at old tormented temple doors

At times even the simple flight
of a pigeon is polite fiction:


Under it fantasies replace each other
while the world's weary history

stretches out along the pavements,
the sky's blue

waiting simply
to be carried by a bird's beak of tears

### Re-enacting an Old Play

The night the prisoner did not choose
triumphs over the distant sky of dawn.
The cycle of hatred between man and man
began with a star standing all alone,
a slow agony betraying itself in its brightness.

Once a friend pushed my seven-year-body
off a tree branch I was sitting on,
and next lay on the ground thinking
what if a crucified god can't stop me
believing in destiny and faith, what then.

This darkness is a net dragging us in a world

of torn gardens so we can't help ourselves
drowning in it. Whatever I was searching for
had revealed something else, and I could hear
the long silent cry of the humiliated star
as history's old home was raised from the dust.

Sometimes I almost think I'm hearing things.
Like tormented church bells, wailing minarets,
sleepwalking rifle fire, psalms in dying men,
and sick snails walking inside themselves.
And the pleas of those who insist
they are serving mankind in the silence
of the kneeling prisoner, waiting
to be shot on the still, desert sands.


## After the Death of a Friend

Grief, and more grief, taking us nowhere.
My mother is wearing a discolored dress
and she's been dead for years now.
Noises of the play-acting buffonery of children
harassing a madman in the street reach me.
Spring flowers break down silently on the hills.
My breath stretches and roams the stiffened fields.
Buried murmurs break loose from the end of a life.

I pick up the tumbler, almost empty, and swallow.
Hiroshima is a myth, I think. And the Kalinganagar dead.
A stab wound pierces the fear of the dark again.

In its shadow-blood the words of dialectic economics
are washed away; there is no urge to the miracle

for the country's landless to light
the split finger-nails of torpid paddy fields.

It's indifference when we let our unseen poor
pass the night chanting prayers in the starvation-light
where laughter rests in parliamentarians mouths.
A second is a breath that doesn't take long to end.

Unsure, 1 look around like last year's calendar
trying to pick out sorrow; memory celebrates
when it finds shadows through flesh,
mourning only the one who leaves a name,


## Behind Closed Windows

Needless to say
our lives are spent behind closed windows.
A queer restlessness deepens
the wrinkles on my forehead.
Nothing else.
Only my skin seems to swim lazily in the air.
I realize it can't
make me move a bit of the world.
I learned to live at my own will
long before.

Around me are the wretched ones;
they don't want love
even when they die off, one by one.
I've come to dislike the world so much
that when my father died
I took the burning face and dropped it

on top of the pile
of crushed-out cigarettes in the ash tray.

I took the Robinson Crusoe
from my last book of innocence
and held it against the light:
all those solitudes
only rammed the condemned lighthouse
to the sky.

Today I awake in my strange bed
in my strange room
without noticing the window
where the darkness of my heart
fumbles near the end of its time.

And because our lives are so hard
and all our myths are killing us,
it's terrible not to bear any malice
for the righteous little moon
that makes me lovesick with each look,
that allows dreams to take over like criminals,
before falling apart,
like reason.

## Ash

Even
the view beyond it
gives away nothing

The stillness
that plays on
with the pulsing of butterflies

Over
the illusive wings
of dawn and dusk

## Hesitant Light

A shaft of stray sunlight
in the littered streets.
The wail of an approaching ambulance
makes the dawn seem unreal.
To the east, geese lumber past
in the impassive half-light.
A man jumps aside to avoid stepping on
some animal's bloody intestines,
and I suddenly remember
the well in which villagers up north
had found seven corpses in the first light.

In a windowless fisherman's shack
a footstep of darkness left behind
longs to take a leap into the infinite.
Someone there sits huddled and waiting
after a petty crime in the night.

Where we go is unimportant.
Life's choices are few.
When someone passes on outward, into thought,
perhaps growing smaller,
he's buried in this earth,

the rise and fold of hills,
the outcrops of rock, the stone skin
of ancient walls, that shelter
the faraway footfalls of secret hierarchies.

Above the ruin of days
another December dawn
crawls along the ground,
in its hesitant light,
but swift and hidden;
to be imprisoned by this thing
that was like a door
that had no walls behind it,
and still held on to the inconceivable
breadth of the world, its sweetness,

its treasures
its ends and its endlessness.


## There Were No Trumpet Blasts

(In memory of the 142 children murdered in Peshawar
on December 16, 2014)

There were no trumpet blasts
through the scarred bony mist that morning

No signs of caged rage

Inheritors of the plaster cast of a land
their child voices rushing out of the long minds
of their liberal laughter

My pain is a want, I realize
not desire

Maybe I live seven lives as I watch
the grimacing wind of my distant present
lead me into a cold dark corridor

Maybe I'd like to see
my left eye pluck out my right
while
between the silence within myself
and that in the high school wall of death

All the voices of history
begin to speak all at once


## A Self Portrait

I have nothing to declare.

But the stifled laughter from my throat
when in a dream I'd held aloft
the triumphant plate with the vanquished head,
severed and bloody and swollen,
a toy lying in the sweet flowery season of youth.
For years I tried hard
to be some kind of hero, but failed,
or there would have been something to say.
Then too, I reasoned to myself,
although I had no need of that
a long eighty years
just innocence hung, a loose and crumpled shirt

upon my lining body
And it left me short of nakedness.

So it went.
At times the shock of seeing life
made me loose direction
as I ran here and there.
There were those who taught me to think
some good would come out of it.
Centuries ago, it was insecurity
that made me peer into the deathlessness of time;
only something like the blood of history,
suddenly magical, suddenly strange,
could reveal a purpose of its dark mind.
I was torn between
the desire to know, and fear of knowing
I didn't realize I had to live in the future
in order to face the sleepless night of the present.
What time of mine faces me now?
Perhaps I do not really need to know.
These hands of mine have terrible memories;
they are always after me.
And every time I look at those hands
that had held up the head on the platter
I see my own.

The urge to wear newer masks
has never ended.
It grows, unnoticed.
To tear the body of perfection from limb to limb
and throw the pieces to an empty dream.
It's no use declaring anything
about the man I perhaps did not know at all:

the faded initials we had once carved
on the weak bark of our faith,
or the grief of finding oneself not chosen
by the object of one's desire;
the magic, the science and the religion
that had broken out
from the loneliness of the exiled self.

The mask has to be worn,
and no one has the impulse not to wear one.
Only something resembling a memory
could measure
what one had lost or gained:
the mask's blindness only revealed
the eyes of an assassin
who had picked up yet another new victim.

## That Evening, Nabaneeta

That evening, in the thin drizzle, when the train
halted at Bidisha Station, both Nabaneeta and I
got down and held the wet earth in our cupped palms.
Our hearts were on tire, simply because once
Jibanananda wrote about it. And Bidisha
floated down into the abyss of the heart's half-light.
It was a good reason for untamed madness. We stood there,
startled by the force
of an inner impatience. The perfect, flawless illusion
of Banalata Sen passed through the long shadow
the stars blur threw over the earth;
a sense of the wholeness of life filled the air.
Soon Nabaneeta fell asleep in her berth like a child.
It was the monsoon month of 1985, an evening

when my fingertips moved to touch Banalata Sen's hair,
caressed it and then lightly stroked her face.

In another evening today we look out; it is all so different.
Lost of its stillness, the evening awakes in a sweat.
It does not dream.
It has a voice that mocks me, secret and persistent.
How quietly it has undressed its human feelings! Where
is the love we felt once? The darkness deepens;
the slogans for revenge have swallowed up the stars.
The breasts of the beaten earth gasp in the savage wind.
Grim-faced hunters return again; elsewhere, a small town
like Bidisha jerks in spasms as its body twists in an effort
to escape the knife. In the trembling, endless darkness
the hunters' faces glow like handsome priests.
And that long lost evening seems a beautiful mistake, Nabaneeta.


## Fable of the First Person

Thrown away from the body I own
even I doubt my identity

Between this race and the next
Between this sentimental song and another

One would only elevate himself
to embody an abrupt tranquility

For the sake of an empty word of faith
Something strange flies the fate of my life

Living in a graveyard without my body
inside the echo of the world's madness

Flapping its minarets is small answer
to the body beating time with severed feet


**Fable of the First Traveller**

These
are those cares
that have left their footprints behind

Anarchic affections that ask
what to do with oneself,
how to go on until tomorrow.

These are the sorrows of today.

Whatever is, is rarely seen.
Each witness is a God
safe inside himself
wanting to face his own surprise

Like iron rails
they shine shamefacedly in moonlight.
The tired heart
begins to walk on them.
I live so little in the future.
But my memory is so full
that I'd like to lose more of it.

## Fable of the First Worshipper

The village temple straddled my heart.
No thunderstorm swept over it,
no cloud poured its tattered light,
no hunger clutched with cold hands
at the naked flowers on its breast.
No one knew he had been betrayed.

I have been here forever. Simple as that.
I never thought each one here
could be made of clay,
and our wounds smeared over our birth.
The village temple straddles my heart.
This voice my sorrows need:
even the ten thousand dead stones
have a lame answer
to the old witch ready to eat the little girl.


## At the Rock Edict of Emperor Ashoka, Dhauli Hill, Odisha, 261 B.C.

Weary is the hand of God
that never reaches this hidden place
of a land's lost morals.
High up the hill, one watches
as the moonlight still scours the dry riverbed
for bodies of the dead in the vain sands
trapped by cries of pain, as the year's pilgrims
trudge the tortured valley of the Daya
in the pride of a singular belief.

Today I find it hard to stand the dividing walls
laid out by those greedy days of battle
and one-eyed men, and the hungry vows of heroism
that shape the nameless crossing of the bridge.
A graveyard without peace is this embroidered
rock with the fading decrees. Unwanted flowers
bloom there in perfect silence, white, alive;
maybe to set free a scent of sadness

I take for an answer to God's hand
hanging somewhere outside my handful of air.

Note: *100,000 of my ancestors were massacred by the
Mauryan Emperor Ashoka in the Kalinga
War, 260-61 BC. Later, Ashoka turned to Buddhism and
issued a number of decrees advocating
non-violence in all spheres of life. Dhauli is on the River
Daya, 25 kilometres from Cuttack,
where I live.*

## End of the Rains in the Hills of Odisha

End of the rains in the hills of Odisha.
No wetness drips now from the trees.
Just a silvery light on the black-green twigs
more like the unapologetic smile on faces of the old
and the ill crowding the merciless temple door.
Lonely, the men crouch over the uncertainties
of the coming night, and a river hums
somewhere, hidden and full of seduction.
And empty voices that follow thoughtlessly where
swift streams rushed past two weeks ago.

Even as the wood pheasants call from the bushes,
here and in the bright, clear air of the land
where both soldiers and gunmen
go on emptying their rifles at each other.

The dark goddess high up on the hill slope
stretches the hours of ugly, bloodied nights,
her eyes the monopoly of death. Long,
dry sighs of worshippers are merely marooned
in the shadows that secure her legend and life.
She is the goddess fetishized by blood,
watching over bamboo and bramble and people
who let themselves be swept from world to world.

Down in a sickly village
a woman trembles to her painful career
as no voice breaks through her open mouth.
And someone close to her feels a tenderness
born out of nowhere, turning speechlessness
and mist into neither darkness nor light.

And now, in a raging harvest,
the tribe celebrates
in the drum-heavy rite of abandon and dance.
But autumn will soon find
the roots of trees and wild cries of men
who must reckon again upon their loves,
under the stare of the Sleepless One;
when dreams do not change,
and men with dreams darker than their evenings
return again and again
to fling their tired, bound bodies
against the eternal river, that husk of hope,

the iron roaring over them and hacking up
the night and the rain.


## Uneasy, in the Silent Night
*for Runu*

Uneasy, here in the silent night.
Blind all along, blind to the real meaning
of death and its life, we come up with a play,
where the actors, with nowhere to turn, simply
palpitate slowly like stars streaming out in the sky.

It's the wounds of your life that look down
at me, uncertain what to do; and your eyes, shut,
leaving, to find another life on another world.
I am the stranger who would hold back his tears,
my spirit conditioned to the actor's body, hard,
disciplined.

And I look for the pain when I lean over
your cold face, as I realize I was using it
to escape whatever it was I was running from.
Perhaps memory, helpless against love or sympathy,
hovering above the ground like rain that never fell.

Among the carnival frenzy in Como, that day,
I saw the fear in your eyes, hugging your chest,
your lips ghosting a smile. You are what you are.
Floating against the sides of this day, oh love,
let the silent night make us love the silence of your love.

## Tomorrow I Could Find Myself Lying about My Life

Fireflies float around the tamarind tree in the rain.
Past summers kneel down to my rain-wet body.

The house sits large and lonely on a half-drunk song.
Desire fixes it with its old rhythms and histories.

Dream children like actors in a play
are ready to drop their roles,
and then become characters they played,
larger than before.

Let them play, Td like to say,
making their moves, as I go on making mine.

I watch a cloud hunt with wet eyes.
Tomorrow I could be lying about my life.

## The Triumph of Things

Things can happen over and over again.
Like putting tuberoses in this vase
and watching them die slowly
without dreams and respect and rain.
Like finding oneself
at the corner of an unknown road,
and wandering through the confusion
of some powerless anonymity.
Sometimes a thing is what it looks like.

It is not a front for something else. Like god.
Time can wear someone's blood for clothing
and be a little unreal,
wondering too if it was seated backward
on a donkey, and incomprehensible after all.
And when things happen again and again,
those we wish would never happen,
how can one love a country, or hate it?
Perhaps man can only fully understand
what he has made himself,
even the stories he retails.
I know how gunshots
sound ominously in the valley
when the reds at sunset in autumn
tint the fields of golden mustard in the hills,
and how I use my love for my country
as a justification for the truth
of feelings patently false.
But is history deliberate,
on one level or another?
And now too, these things cannot make me
give up my large world
where freedom can be tied to a stake and burnt,
with something like a butterfly
irreplaceable in the garden, and time
unable to distinguish machine gun fire
from the trot of the handsome prince on horseback
in a lost land heard or in childhood.

## Tales We Have Always Heard

The slaughterhouse is more than stone slabs,
more than the witchcraft of blades.
The cloud of homecoming;
how long have we to wait for its rain
to build the walls around us?

The girl in the tight red dress
walks past her own images
as she pushes away the vast deserts
into the sacred oasis of her coming night.

Bent over itself,
is this sky in the last rise of hope
thrashing around like a beached fish
on the noose of a dying sun.

There are these tales we've always heard:
of the river that has seduced us into sailing,
of the rainbow's swash that would bring
a long emptiness back to life for us,
and the steps of the dead
that revoke the vow to the murdered girl
only to sink among the paving stones.

Now we sit in each other's living rooms
assuring ourselves that we are still of this world,
as compassion and tenderness
slip from a sinking Titanic out of yesterday,
happier with their disguises in the nest of our tales.

## A Burning Ground by the River

Spreads of weed and grass
No marked grave that I could find
in this burning ground by the river
I sit here for a time, to weep a memory,
thoughtless for peace.
If I stay on in the ashes of a thousand years,
it would strengthen my feeling
that I was the one
chosen to walk only by myself,
and that I might go further,
parallel life crosses on my worn palms.
Today the world won't wait as I do,
it dies in the distance,
arrogant red sun among the clouds.
Id hardly speak: the murdered girl
who was cremated here last week
had left behind the silence of a nameless life
as a defence against the freedom
that goes on to make the power of the world.
All the groping in my mind
for the thought to be proud of something
something where, I'd feel protected, and free.

And as I sat there, it came. A lost moonlight.
It played around the ashes. It had a face,
looming larger as it approached.
Every look seemed to be an attempt on my life.
The wing couldn't escape being choked
by the ashes. I couldn't help notice
the cold uniform of the moonlight.
It took me years to walk back home.

## Signs

Something glances at me over my shoulder.
What does it see?
Old clothes, familiar days, bright instincts,
and those intimate little things that count in the end.
Or does it hear those silent footsteps
that remind one of the hushed noises
of a hundred settled birds at dusk?
Maybe it feels the tight curl of my fingers
in my pocket.
To tell the truth, a voice inside
calls for help still. The childish sorrow
leaps at me like a cat, when I feel
I have become someone else. My lite cannot remember
when between the all and the nothing, I found
everything the opposite of what I had imagined.
It recalls how once it watched over
the morals of a nation, looking to an uneasy future.
I drift past prisons, their torture chambers
and my rage against a distant past.
And drag myself away both from beauty queens
and mangled lepers, the religious grandeur of priests,
fanatical in love with the secret scents of their bodies,
while they risk their keyless farewells.
Memories heavy with weariness,
that serve not as heroes
but hostages that left no room for compromise.
One begins a day by looking at oneself
in the glass. It becomes a challenge
as if the image, unable to bear its stillness,
didn't know which way to look,
almost losing its perfection and its balance.

Is this a symptom people can't bear to see
the sign that is able to change them:
That the sudden stillness drags its hunt
back to the month of the cave?
Before, the hand, out of nowhere,
touches the shoulder?
The strange grief of the blue in the sky
peers down at me. The calmness my father
showed once is a thousand miles away.

## My City: Poem One

Everything seems so familiar:
The roads hanging onto their worn crutches
The dry, sulking riverbeds
The flowery tops of rich young girls
Fluttering like victory flags
And the story of Shabnam
The raped sixteen-year-old
Who disappeared from Dargha Bazar
That still clouds the necklaces
Of festival lights
Everything is so familiar
I feel I know where I'm going
That I want to sing loudly into the darkness
I sing because I'm afraid of my heart's cry
Because I steal away like a thief
From those dying from jaundice and dengue
Because I carry the love with me
Leaving the farewell behind
And because of the sorrowful bare temple
From which God drifts away without echo
In the flat, toothless city

Today I know well
Those dogs who bark and fight it out
In the roads between the houses

I know the children
Who kick at their coming years
As they chase and curse
The mad women in those streets

And I know the good clean smell
Of the new morning
As it stands on the edge of the city
From another murder
That is a cloying answer
In the crowded streets of Sheikh Bazar

## My City: Poem Two

I haven't slept all night
Because
The night's been lying beside me
Stretched out on the mat.

So meek, this night.
I dare not disturb it.
Yet, at times unnoticed
It lifts itself up
And stalks through the dark
Like a bird of prey.

An untold bit of news
In the city's daily newspaper
Plucks out
The heart of the waiting dawn.

## On India's Independence Day

A day of light rain
where nothing comes and goes.

I pick up a little earth, smell it.
Does earth everywhere scent its wetness?
Sixtynine years back, something
lost itself and fell the whole way.

It was then that another dark rain
blew tenderness out of our lives.
Freedom! Our leaders shouted at the celebrations.
Freedom! We cried as the Prime Minister wiped his brow.

Nothing is the same anymore,
not the way the rainbow flew past the rain
to dry its eyes in the rainbow's house,
not our love, where we lived without knowing,

As we sailed joyfully
between this world and the next,
nor memory that hung like a precious charm.
Even the silence of rice fields today

Sounds like a factory's dumb, red hum.
But what do I look for in such a day?
For a little old man who still sits
on the keel of the old day fishing for truth?

Or for the white paper bag in my hand
that weighs almost nothing,
but with a scream stuck deep inside,
A scream so frightful that I can't get it out?

## The Ruins of the World

Another day falls into nowhere.
The past walks alone.
On this street too:
just the memory of a journey
that is lost before I step on it.

A poor thin salesgirl is this India,
her face above the toothless
jewelry tray display of her past
more a moving wash, hung out to dry
in the indifference of the world.

Grim hillsides preserved behind glass,
of human hair and teeth,
of spectacles and sobbing shoes,
of the pain of pain in a distant land
is story enough.

In my country there is a village too.
It has a field for the dead.
At one spot ashes keep flying out

through the ground. They look like
grinning soldiers with clean uniforms
and three legs each.
I've not seen that land. Or the field.
Time, keeps feeding on itself,
because it is always moving.
The few red stains in the sky
I see every evening never disturb me.
this silent night might lose its way again
and I wouldn't know it.
Here at home, I think of reaching home.
And I can't say why I remember
the thief who refused to believe.
And the second who wanted to be left alone.

## BLACK EAGLE BOOKS

www.blackeaglebooks.org
info@blackeaglebooks.org

Black Eagle Books, an independent publisher, was founded as
a nonprofit organization in April, 2019. It is our mission to
connect and engage the Indian diaspora and the world at large
with the best of works of world literature published on a
collaborative platform, with special emphasis on
foregrounding Contemporary Classics and New Writing.